TOBET4ENGAGE!
A Christ-Centered Guide to Happy Marriage

What a wonderful adventure you are heading toward: a journey you will travel together as companions— as spouses; a journey that will last for the rest your lives. How well have you packed?

Engagement should be far more than just a time to plan for a wedding. St. John Paul II saw the crucial need for all engaged persons to "test" the truth of their love by reflecting upon who they really are as persons, who their future spouse really is, and how the two of them together understand the vocation of marriage.

He invited each engaged person to ponder questions like,
- "What does it really mean to be a human person, body and soul?"
- "What should our 'reciprocity' as a husband and wife look like?"
- "How will we form and sustain a mature 'we' and not just live together as two egoistic 'I's'?"

We hope this marriage preparation program will provide you an opportunity to answer important questions like these. We have drawn from St. John Paul II's Theology of the Body (TOB), a deep exploration of the meaning of the human body, especially in the context of marital love. May it guide you as you ponder what it truly means to commit yourselves to each other in that lifelong adventure known as the vocation of marriage.

—Monica Ashour, MTS; M Hum and TOBET Members

Table of Contents

INTRODUCTION
The Wonder of Marriage
Marriage in the Plan of God

PART 1
The Gift of Love is FREE
Becoming my Real Self, My "I," so I Can Love

PART 2
The Gift of Love is FULL
Giving my Real Self for Communion: Becoming "We"

PART 3
The Gift of Love is FAITHFUL
"We" Living the Sacramentality of Marriage and the Meaning of Sex

PART 4
The Gift of Love is FRUITFUL
Our Love Overflows into the Lives of Others

PART 5
The Gift of Love Forms FAMILY
"We" Becoming Holy: Living the Truth as Family

CONCLUSION
Marriage as the Mirror of the Gospel
Bringing Christ to the World through Marriage

How to use the Theology of the Body Marriage Preparation:

Open-Mind
TOB is a fantastic view of the person, marriage, sex, and family life! We hope that you are able to set aside any preconceived ideas of Catholic doctrine and enter into this message of hope.

Open-Vision
More than a gift for one's own happiness, marriage is an opportunity for sacrificial love which affects not just the spouses, but their children, the Church, and all of society.

Open-Ended
This book is an introduction to the fantastic insights of St. John Paul's Theology of the Body in a simple, accessible way— to be used in various ways: in a marriage prep setting, ongoing dialogue for couples, before and throughout your marriage, for young adults, even for older teens.

Open-Heart
Each of us is in need of ongoing conversion to Christ. May this book be a means for deepening your love together.

Open-Dialogue

We suggest you journal and/or formulate your own ideas and then discuss them as a couple.

For those who want to delve deeper, please visit tobet.org and see pg. 77 of this book for more resources.

A note from the members of TOBET:

The content presented in this book is primarily from Pope Saint John Paul II's teachings—his *Theology of the Body* and other works—but also from the personal experiences of the members of TOBET (Theology of the Body Evangelization Team) as we have interacted with the words of the St. John Paul in our lives. Each of us in his or her own way has been shown the beauty of marriage through the life-changing, breath-taking lens of the Theology of the Body. This teaching has shown us the magnitude of what it means to be a married person, especially in the true wonders of sexuality and the depth of meaning of marital intercourse.

We are from different walks of life, of different ethnicities, and have come to our appreciation of the Theology of the Body through different trials. We all are sinners, yet we continue to repent and live as best we can. Some of us were hooked on pornography. Some of us were in codependent relationships. Some of us cohabited. Some of us had children out of wedlock. Some of us resisted such sins but repressed sexual desire. Some of us are recovering alcoholics and drug addicts. Some of us are divorced. Some of us were womanizers. Some of us picked up men at bars. Some of us contracepted. Some of us experienced same-sex attraction. Some of us were sexually abused and then acted out promiscuously. Some of us have had abortions. In a word… We are sinners. We resonate with what Pope Francis said in identifying himself: "I am a sinner."

Most of us are now in good, secure marriages thanks to our understanding of these teachings, though, of course, we still have the typical struggles of life, and still work to see our spouse and children with a reverence that fully acknowledges the deep mystery of their personhood.

We share these teachings with you not in a judgmental way, but with the intention of giving you the tools which have helped us. Knowing our brokenness, we begged God for Mercy. Finally, we allowed His Mercy and Healing to break through. This came with a personal encounter with Christ and His Church—which mainly happened because we heard the message of the Theology of the Body. **It changed our lives.**

This program was designed by us sinners for sinners…in need of mercy, forgiveness, and grace…continually striving to be the best we can be. It is based on our experience before receiving healing, as well as after Christ touched our lives through the Theology of the Body, giving us hope and healing. Our intention is to give you tools to help you and your future marriage and family.

We have given Monica Ashour, Co-founder of TOBET, permission to give you our contact information if you would like to talk with any of us regarding our personal journeys. If you would like to dialogue regarding any of the issues we worked through, Monica knows each of us and can direct you to the person whose life experience best fits yours, in case you need a sounding board. Most of us are not counselors, but we can listen and advise. If you'd like, please contact Monica at info@tobet.org and know that your identity will be kept sacred and private.

— TOBETers, Old and New Members, 2001 to present

INTRODUCTION
The Wonder of Marriage
MARRIAGE IN THE PLAN OF GOD

In the Beginning there was…

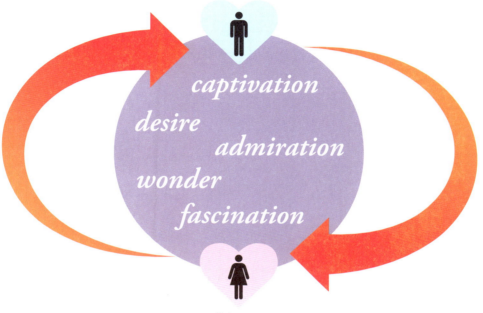

Based on Song of Songs and *TOB* 1-23; 108. © Copyright 2014 by Monica Ashour. All rights reserved.

"I am my beloved's and he is mine."
Song of Songs 6:3

How wonderful it is that you are in love!

You are being drawn to each other into something bigger than yourselves; you are *in* love, "inside" of a great mystery. We will be journeying in this book to take a look at your new relationship in the broadest context of love as you continue to discern your call to marriage. May the wonder and fascination you have for each other deepen to a confident, lifelong love. The gift of self—none other than love—will see you through.

1. When was the first time you realized you were in love with your future spouse?

"Set me as a seal on your heart, for love is as strong as death."

Song of Songs 8:6.

Seeing: Man with Eyes and Woman with Heart

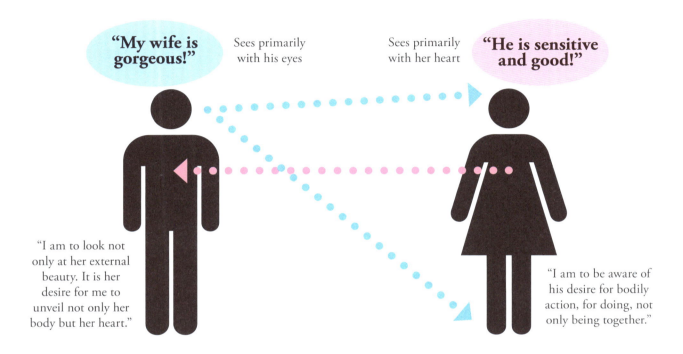

Based on *TOB* 109:1. © Copyright 2013 by Monica Ashour. All rights reserved.

Men and women experience reality in different ways and come at love differently as a man or as a woman. St. John Paul gives great insights in his Theology of the Body, helping us to see that the man is more sensitive to the physical and the woman to the emotional. This is not good or bad—it is what it is. Knowing these truths will help you understand each other, strengthening your relationship.

1. Pope John Paul says the man sees mostly with the eyes—being more physically-charged—and the woman sees mostly with the heart—being more emotionally-charged. How can knowing these realities help you to understand each other and appreciate the other's gifts?

2. How can these realities become weaknesses and sources of conflict in your marriage?
   What can you do to work through the weaknesses and conflicts?

"… love unleashes a special experience of the beautiful, which focuses on what is visible, but at the same time, it involves the entire person. The experience of beauty gives rise to pleasure, which is reciprocal."

Pope John Paul II, *TOB* 108:3

What is Love?

Superficial Understanding of Love	What Real Love Is
Entitlement	Free Gift
Fun times only	Sacrifice
Feeling	Decision
Fair-weather friend	Journey
When it feels good	Totally in
Expecting perfection	Forgiving

© Copyright 2014 by Monica Ashour. All rights reserved.

Many messages in movies and other media give us a superficial depiction of love. Man meets woman. Woman meets man. They fall in love and are always happy. Love is simply a good feeling. No sacrifice, no vows, no journey in tough times together. Just butterflies and roses with no thorns. It is true, though, that Prince Charming and Snow White can marry and live happily ever after ...as long as they give the true gift of self—love—in a sacrificial, demanding, and fulfilling way. You can live your own fairytale, but there are evil monsters, magic, and madmen out there, trying to keep you apart. But love, true love, conquers even death.

1. Outside of a romantic relationship, when have you experienced someone loving you sacrificially? Was it hard for you to *receive* such a gift of self?

2. When have you *given* the gift of self sacrificially, even though it was exceedingly hard?

3. What are some specific experiences that you know your future spouse has had that are evidence that he or she understands sacrificial love?

4. Have you considered that at different moments in your marital journey, you will have harder times where one of you will have to pick up your cross and make an even greater sacrificial gift? Are you confident you will do that? Are you confident your future spouse has that capability?

5. Is there any way out of marriage?

"Even if *eros* is at first mainly covetous and ascending, a fascination for the great promise of happiness, in drawing near to the other, it is less and less concerned with itself, increasingly seeks the happiness of the other, is concerned more and more with the beloved, bestows itself and wants to 'be there for' the other. The element of *agape* thus enters into this love, for otherwise *eros* is impoverished and even loses its own nature."

Pope Benedict XVI, *God Is Love* 7

INTRO

"God is love."
1 John 4:8

God's Inner Life of Love

Father
Holy Spirit
Son

Created by Dr. Margaret Turek. © Copyright 2013 by Monica Ashour. All rights reserved.

We might ask ourselves *why* we believe the things we do about love. Why do we think that love puts the other first, is given freely and completely, etc.?

As believers, we find the answer in the nature of God. The Mystery of the Trinity—that God is three distinct Persons who give the gift of self to each other from all eternity—is the blueprint of all love.

Love as the gift of self is represented in this book by arrows of reciprocal giving and receiving, which is always open to another. In this diagram, the Father and Son give the gift of self to each other, and the Holy Spirit, Who always existed, is the "fruit" or bond of their union.

God's Blueprint of Love for the Universe:
Giving / Receiving / Fruit

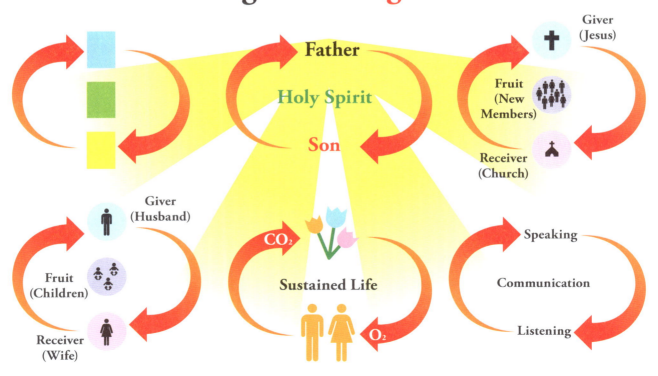

© Copyright 2014 by Monica Ashour. All rights reserved.

TOBET4ENGAGED

Your Marriage in the Big Picture

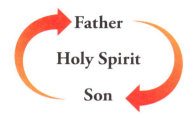 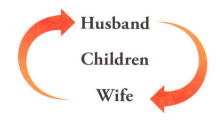 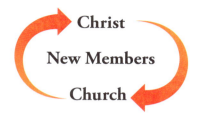

© Copyright 2014 by Monica Ashour. All rights reserved.

ALL GOOD RELATIONSHIPS REFLECT GOD'S ETERNAL NATURE.

The Trinity
A Person-to-Person, indissoluble relationship of love for fruitful communion.

Marriage
A person-to-person, indissoluble relationship of love for fruitful communion.

Christianity
A Person-to-person, indissoluble relationship of love for fruitful communion.

In this analogy, it is important to note that God is the "blueprint," setting up the pattern of love for all relationships, not vice versa. We should not put human terms on God but realize God's reality is stamped into our humanity.

You and your future spouse are reading this book because you are preparing for a lifelong journey of lasting love. Love lasts when its basis is in God. So, the more you know about God's own inner life of love, the more light is shed on your future marriage. Similarly, the more you know about the union of Christ and the Church, the more you will be able to love each other. Of course, we are not perfect, but in our daily struggles, looking to God as the model of love can help direct our actions and attitude.

This diagram may seem like rocket science, but it is not. *All l*ove entails the gift of self in giving, in receiving, in reciprocating, and in the fruit—the consequence of such love.

On a very simple level, consider this: Ladies, your fiancé gave the gift of himself while on his knee, *giving* you a ring. You gave the gift of self by *receiving* his vulnerable gift by saying, "Yes!" and reciprocating by *giving* a hug and your fiancé *received* your hug. And the *fruit* is love flourishing which affects all of us! We are glad you are getting married!

Or guys: Your fiancée gave the gift of self by baking and *giving* you cookies. You gave the gift of self by *receiving*—eating!—the cookies. You reciprocated by *giving* a compliment: "They're delicious!", and she *received* the compliment, which resulted in the *fruit* of a strengthened relationship.

1. When did you experience today this pattern of giving, receiving, reciprocity, and fruit?
   What are other times in your life that you experienced this fruitful love?

2. Which is harder for you: giving, receiving, reciprocating, or being open to fruit?
   Which is harder for your future spouse?

"[Marriage is] a sign that efficaciously transmits in the visible world the invisible mystery hidden in God from eternity. And this is the mystery of Truth and Love, the mystery of divine life…."
— Pope John Paul II, *TOB* 19:4

All Love Comes from the Heart of the World

Based on Fr. Hans Urs von Balthasar's *The Heart of the World* and *Humanae Vitae*, 9. © Copyright 2014 by Monica Ashour. All rights reserved.

Jesus says, "This is my commandment, that you love one another as I have loved you."
John 15:12

As Christians, we know God is fully revealed in Christ. So when we look to God for the nature of love, our gaze is on Jesus, and in Him we see Love, given to us *freely, fully, faithfully,* and *fruitfully*. We see that if His sacrificial gift of love were not *freely* given, it would not be love, but a coerced tragedy; if it were not *full*, it would be a half-hearted mimic of love; if it were not *faithful*, we could not put our trust in Him; and if it were not *fruitful*, we would not be saved.

With God's grace, we seek to enter into the standard of true love shown to us by Christ. We will continue to journey in this book, taking a look at true love always containing the **Four F's** of *free, full, faithful,* and *fruitful*. Even though some may say that love, and thus marriage, cannot last forever, we as believers know such a skeptical view is not true, for God's love is eternal. All true marriages enter into God's eternal love.

1. What are some practical steps you can take to ensure that your married life is based on the true and lasting love of the four F's?

PART 1

The Gift of Love is FREE

BECOMING MY REAL SELF, MY "I," SO I CAN LOVE

The Body Matters!

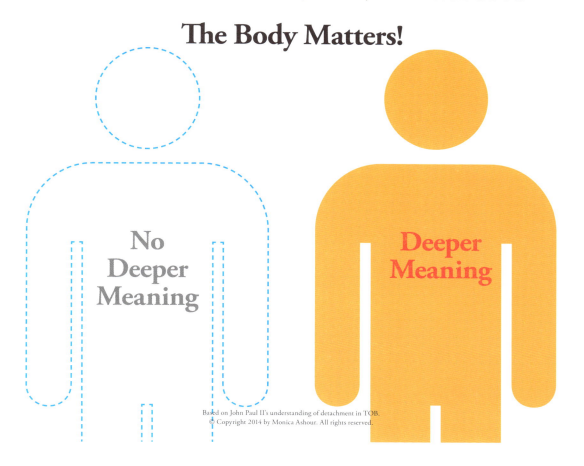

Based on John Paul II's understanding of detachment in TOB.
© Copyright 2014 by Monica Ashour. All rights reserved.

Have you ever thought of the significance of the body and bodily actions? When you see a body, you know that's a person, "no matter how small," so says Dr. Seuss. Or when you see your future spouse gaze into your eyes, you know that has a depth of *meaning*: "I'm in love with you." Even more simply, when a mom and dad smile at their newborn—that bodily expression means "It is good that you are here!" These *visible* signs—the body, gazing into eyes, a smile—have a deep, unchanging, invisible meaning. We call this the Sacramental or Incarnational View of Reality. This fancy term simply means that the body *matters*…matter *matters*… it has special *meaning*.

Four movies, *Avatar*, *Inception*, *Surrogate*, and *Her*, although well-produced, depict the modern viewpoint of the body—as an empty shell, with no meaning, with "reality" taking place away from one's body. In contrast, as we continue to try to understand marriage more deeply, we will see that the body has *tremendous meaning* and *significance*. Let's take a look at the male body and female body and their *meaning*.

"…The highest affirmation of man [is] the affirmation of the body given life by the Spirit."
Pope John Paul II, *The Redeemer of Man*, 18

"And the word became flesh and dwelt among us." John 1:14

Language of the Male Body

What does the male body communicate?
"Protect, Provide, Pursue"

Physical characteristic	Meaning
Generally stronger with larger bone structure	Protect others who are smaller (especially women and children)
Metabolism faster than female	Endurance to hunt or gather for providing
Shoulders broader than female	Strength for bearing burdens and elevating others
Thinking tends to stay on one hemisphere of the brain	Task oriented; focused on fixing things and solving problems
Larger amygdala in the brain, which regulates sexual behavior	Greater sexual drive
Sexual organ—exterior	Action-oriented; designed to initiate love

© Copyright 2014 by Monica Ashour. All rights reserved.

"Have you not read that from the beginning the Creator 'made them male and female'?"
—Jesus, Matthew 19:4

"Each of the sexes is an image of the power and of the tenderness of God, with equal dignity though in a different way." CCC 2335

"The words 'masculinity' and 'femininity,' …. have been reduced from archetypes to stereotypes…. The main fault in the old stereotypes was their too-tight connection between sexual being and social doing, their tying of sexual identity to social roles, especially for women: the feeling that it is somehow unfeminine to be a doctor, lawyer, or politician. But the antidote to this illness is not confusing sexual identities but locating them in our being rather than in our doing."
Peter Kreeft, *Everything You Ever Wanted to Know about Heaven*, 119

The male body has meaning and the female body has meaning. If we take matter seriously, we see that it conveys and brings about a hidden reality. That's the definition of a sacrament—an outward sign that conveys and brings about an inward reality.

So, we can say the body is like a "sacrament" of the person—a visible sign of the invisible, spiritual reality of the person. In other words, "The body 'speaks' a language," meaning that it has meaning.

What do these truths have to do with your upcoming marriage? The answer: you can come to know each other more completely by focusing on the body and its meaning. We are not "ghosts in a machine." We are the integration of body and soul.

Language of the Female Body

What does the female body communicate?
"Hiding, inviting, exciting!"

Physical characteristic	Meaning
Beautiful with curves and swerves	To draw and captivate
Wider pelvis than male	Capacity to receive others
Breasts	To nurture and to excite
Womb	To conceive, support, and protect new life
Thinking tends to cross both hemispheres of the brain	People oriented; focused on the big picture; good at multi-tasking
Larger limbic cortex in the brain, responsible for regulating emotions	Stronger emotional drive
Sexual organ—interior	Being-oriented with deeper interior life; designed to receive love

© Copyright 2014 by Monica Ashour. All rights reserved.

For you women to understand that your future husband is not "hard-wired" in his brain—physiologically speaking—to multi-task, then you won't expect him to do as you do: cook a meal, while simultaneously disciplining your two year old, while simultaneously speaking to your friend on the phone!

And men, you won't launch into fixing the problems your future wife shares with you since you realize that her larger limbic cortex, along with her monthly hormonal changes, sometimes means she just wants you to listen and hold her!

It is true that we are MORE than biological impulses; we have freedom. Nevertheless, the body has a theology—a deep meaning within it.

1. What strikes you about the meaning of the male body and the meaning of the female body?
2. How can this "sacramental understanding" of the male body and female body help you know each other better?
3. What is the difference between knowing the true language of the body and falling into mere gender stereotypes?

"A man shall leave his father and mother and cling to his wife."
Genesis 2:24

The "Sacramental View of Reality" means that the visible has deep meaning. This is especially true for the body, and thus for marriage. Certain bodily actions mean certain things. St. John Paul says, "The body, and only the body, is capable of making visible the invisible realities: the spiritual and the divine." TOB 19:4

The Significance of the Word *Sister*
Based on *"I love you, my sister, my bride."* — Song of Songs 4:9

"Bone of my bone." Gen 2:23

"[All of history is determined by…] who she will be for him and he for her."
TOB 43:7

Based on Song of Songs and *TOB* 109:3-110:4. © Copyright 2014 by Monica Ashour. All rights reserved.

In this book we discuss the many differences between the sexes and their underlying meaning. But beneath the truth underlying those differences lies the common humanity of both sexes. We are equally persons, standing before each other on the same level. To see each other in such a fashion is crucial in having a solid relationship. Our first test of love is to ensure that we are treating our beloved with the respect due to an equal, as a brother or a sister. Such lovers will not lord themselves over their spouse or cower in fear but will squarely face each other in confidence.

This is especially true for believers. We know that in the sight of God our Creator, we are equal, as God's own children. And for Christians, we know ourselves as brothers and sisters in Christ with equal dignity in the Church.

The Scripture "I love you my sister, my bride" may sound weird in this context, but… it says succinctly that we belong to each other through thick and thin like a family, we have equal dignity, though distinct as a man or woman, and that we are to love, never use, each other. This starts with seeing each other properly: as a brother or a sister.

"As Brothers and Sisters we learn to share, challenge, support, belong, be friends, and resolve conflicts."   Dr. Bob Schuchts, *Sexual Wholeness: Restoring the Glory*, 40

How Do You Approach Persons and Things?

Persons	Things
Are to be loved	May be used
Are not to be controlled	Can be controlled
Are subjects of their own lives	Can be objectified
Make their own choices	Have no choice
Are free	Have no freedom
Are unpredictable	Are static
Are mysterious	Can be categorized

© Copyright 2013 by Monica Ashour. All rights reserved.

"The only *proper* response to a person is *love*," says Saint John Paul. Each and every person we encounter deserves a response of love—the stranger, bank teller, waiter, the homeless person, a teacher, a person who experiences same-sex attraction, the saint, the prisoner, your future in-laws!—every person you encounter deserves a response of love. This is especially true of your spouse, the person you encounter most.

Saint John Paul also gives a compelling depiction of the opposite of love. He says the opposite of love is not hatred; the opposite of love is *using* another.

We are to use things, not people. People are to be loved.

Nowadays, the media depicts people jumping straight into sexual relationships, skipping over life-long, committed belonging, and they call that love. The Church sees love differently. We know that no good brother would lust after his own sister or vice versa. TOB challenges us to develop a proper way of seeing one's beloved as a person to love, not as an object to be used.

1. Have you ever thought of loving your future spouse as you would a sibling?
   How does such a loving vision of the other protect the relationship from falling into use?

2. In what ways have you been tempted to use your future spouse? How can you avoid those temptations?
   In what ways do you anticipate being able to reverence and love your spouse as a person? How can you strengthen those behaviors?

3. How can you make sure you see each other as *persons*—including in the area of sexuality—so as to safeguard love now and throughout your marriage?

"Only a person can love and only a person can be loved."

Pope John Paul II, *The Dignity and Vocation of Women, 29*

> *"Do not conform to the pattern of this world, but be transformed by the renewal of your minds. Then you will be able to test what is God's will, what is good, pleasing and perfect."*
>
> Romans 12:2

Spousal Meaning of the Body

Selfish	Spousal
Use (lust)	Gift (love)
Directed to me	Ordered toward union (giving and receiving love)
My pleasure	Your good, my good, and our good
Keeping my options open	Making a commitment
Looking out for myself	Looking out for us
"Test drive"	"I am yours, and you are mine, forever."

Based on *TOB* 27:1. © Copyright 2014 by Monica Ashour. All rights reserved.

"Man cannot live without love. He remains a being that is incomprehensible for himself, his life is senseless, if love is not revealed to him, if he does not encounter love."

Pope John Paul II, *The Redeemer of Man*, 10

Inter-Dependency vs. Co-Dependency

*A co-dependent person believes his/her happiness
comes only from one particular person.*

Co-Dependency "Breaking"	Inter-Dependency "Bending"
Only one person is the focus of the relationship; the other's beliefs and desires are irrelevant or unknown	Each "I" is secure in his/her personhood; each reverences his/her own beliefs as well as the other's
Decisions are based on one person's wants or schedule while the other's needs are not considered	Decisions are based on the good of each person within the context of the relationship
One person is typically seen in an idolized way; the other is typically taken for granted	Both see each other with mutual reverence and awe
One person usually pours out problems and joys; the other takes on these problems and neglects his/her own	Supportive, mutual sharing of problems, joys, and day-to-day experiences
Often without realizing it, one typically uses the other, while the other lets him/herself be used	Careful reflection on the part of both to ensure mutual gift of self, free of selfishness and use
Lacking of proper "solitude" with no distinct "I"	Enriched with "double-solitude" with two distinct "I's"

© Copyright 2015 by Monica Ashour. All rights reserved.

"Be subordinate to one another out of reverence for Christ."
Eph. 5:21

"Sexuality, by means of which a man and woman give themselves to one another through the acts which are proper and exclusive to spouses, is not something simply biological, but concerns the innermost being of the human person as such.

It is realized in a truly human way only if it is an integral part of the love by which a man and woman commit themselves to one another until death."

The Role of the Christian Family in the Modern World, 11

The "spousal" meaning of the body simply means that you are following the "blueprint" of God's love by being a *gift* to each other. By giving yourself to your spouse and reciprocally receiving the gift of self your spouse offers, you build a fruitful friendship with each other. That is, one person is not doing *all of the giving* or *all of the receiving*. If you find that this tilted pattern is present in your relationship, then take a look and see if your love has been tainted by co-dependency.

We should also notice that the goal is not *in*dependence—whereby we live side-by-side—but *inter*-dependence where we enter into each other's life.

1. Looking back on my past relationships, do I find that some were co-dependent relationships? Does my future spouse tends toward co-dependency? What did that look like? Why did it happen?

2. Which row(s) of the table above do we, as a couple, need to work on the most?

3. What are our strengths regarding inter-dependency?

TOBET4**ENGAGED**

Is My "I" Bodily Growing?

"… each one of you knows how to keep his own body with holiness and reverence."
1 Thess 4:4

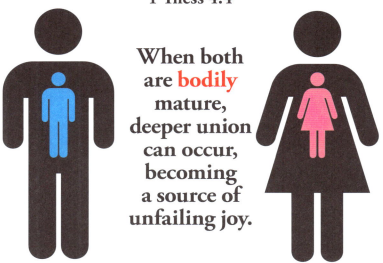

When both are **bodily** mature, deeper union can occur, becoming a source of unfailing joy.

Am I physically addicted to alcohol, drugs, sex, or other things?

Do I treat my body with proper reverence, without glorifying it?

Do I recognize that the body is integral to salvation and holiness?

Based on Pope John Paul II's "Outline of Conjugal Spirituality," *TOB* 131-132. © Copyright 2014 by Monica Ashour. All rights reserved.

SELF-MASTERY CHECKLIST: PHYSICAL HEALTH

1. Am I intentional in exercising, eating properly, enjoying nature, caring for the earth, etc.?
2. Do I show others I love them by being *bodily* present, without distractions (cell phones, iPad, etc.)?
3. Do I work on the Corporal Works of Mercy? (Feed the Poor, Clothe the Naked, Visit the Imprisoned, Shelter the Homeless, Visit the Sick, Feed the Hungry, Give Drink to the Thirsty, Ransom the Captive, Bury the Dead)
4. Are my bodily looks an idol for me? Does my physical health supersede all other things? (spending too many hours on/too much thought about the body)
5. Is the body not important at all? Do I neglect my physical health or not care about my looks? (not enough time spent on attire, health—appearance does not matter)
6. Am I aware of the physiological responses that sexual desire produces? Do I recognize my initial desire is not sinful, but then practice self-mastery so that sexual impulses do not lead to lust?

"Therefore glorify God in your body…"
1 Corinthians 6:20

Is My "I" Emotionally Growing?

"When Jesus saw her weeping… he was deeply moved… Jesus wept."
Jn 11:33-35

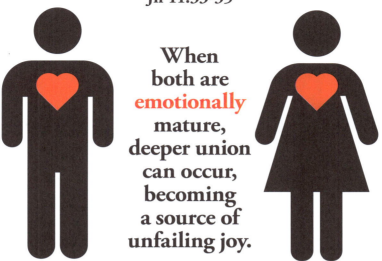

When both are **emotionally** mature, deeper union can occur, becoming a source of unfailing joy.

Have I faced my own brokenness?

Have I, through prayer (and counseling if necessary) experienced Jesus' healing?

Do I strive to have self-mastery over my weaknesses so that I can love fully?

_{Based on Pope John Paul II's "Outline of Conjugal Spirituality," *TOB* 131-132. © Copyright 2014 by Monica Ashour. All rights reserved.}

SELF-MASTERY CHECKLIST: EMOTIONAL HEALTH

1. Do I allow negative experiences from childhood/teenage years to dictate my actions?
2. Do I manipulate others in order to get my way, sometimes without even being aware of it?
3. Have I identified the areas where my emotional "hot buttons" are pushed, and do I know how to govern my emotions in a proper way?
4. Do my parents unduly influence my decisions/moods now in my adult life?
5. Do I have proper boundaries with others without falling into selfishness?
6. Am I addicted to anything? (video games, internet, Hollywood tabloids, sports, people, pornography, TV, shopping, food, gambling, gossip, reading as an escape, social media, etc.)
7. Am I aware of the gifts and faults of those closest to me, so as to accept them and respond lovingly?
8. Do I allow my emotions to have space to "breathe," allowing myself to feel and acknowledge them, or am I afraid of them?
9. Do I hold grudges or am I quick to understand and forgive?

"You have ravished my heart, my sister, my bride."
Song of Songs 4:9

Is My "I" Spiritually Growing?

"For the one who unites himself with the Lord is one with Him in spirit."
1 Cor 6:17

Do I take seriously the responsibility of spiritual leadership?

When both are spiritually mature, deeper union can occur, becoming a source of unfailing joy.

Do I trust my future husband to lead us spiritually?

Is God the center of my life? Do I make weekly Mass attendance a priority?

Do I seek to encounter Jesus in a personal way?

Based on Pope John Paul II's "Outline of Conjugal Spirituality," *TOB* 131-132. © Copyright 2014 by Monica Ashour. All rights reserved.

SELF-MASTERY CHECKLIST: SPIRITUAL HEALTH

1. Do I foster a prayer time? Do I pray with my future spouse?
2. Do I practice the Spiritual Works of Mercy? (To Instruct the Ignorant, Counsel the Doubtful, Admonish the Sinner; Bear Wrongs Patiently, Forgive Offenses Willingly, Comfort the Afflicted, Pray for the Living and the Dead)
3. Do I have time for silence so I can listen to the Lord, or is some sort of media always on?
4. Am I afraid of God's will, or do I actively seek it out?
5. Do I have trusted friends who know the faith and help me to live out my spiritual journey?
6. Do I set a good example for others regarding faith in God?
7. Do I go to Confession regularly, especially if I am in the state of mortal sin?
8. Do I go to Mass to encounter Christ and to receive strength to love?
9. Have I reflected on the rift that sin creates within me, between God and me, between others and me, between nature and me? Do I seek to counter sin with sacrificial love?
10. Do I realize that God loves me and wants what is best for me and my future spouse?

"If we live in the Spirit, let us also follow the Spirit."
Gal 5:25

1 FREE

*"Remain in me, as I also remain in you.
No branch can bear fruit by itself;
it must remain in the vine.
Neither can you bear fruit unless you remain in me."*

John 15:4

A Solid Marriage Is Built on Knowing Christ

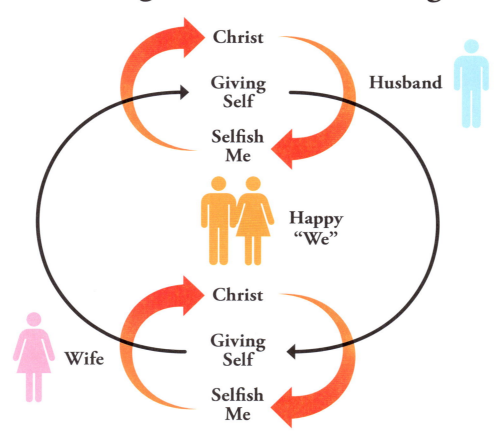

Based on Eph 5:21 and *TOB* 89-90; *TOB* 128:3. © Copyright 2014 by Monica Ashour. All rights reserved.

"Remember that there are no victim-less crimes, that every time you weaken your soul, you weaken the Body of Christ and every member of it, including those you love the most."

Peter Kreeft, *Catholic Christianity*, 256

1. Have you ever thought of the impact having a personal relationship with Christ (or not having one) will have on your marriage? What are your thoughts and feelings concerning this?

2. Do you think your future spouse believes one's relationship with God (or lack thereof) will affect your future marriage? Will there be tension or a deep security regarding living the life of faith in your future marriage?

PART 2

The Gift of Love is FULL

GIVING MY REAL SELF FOR COMMUNION: BECOMING "WE"

The Meaning of the Husband-Wife Relationship

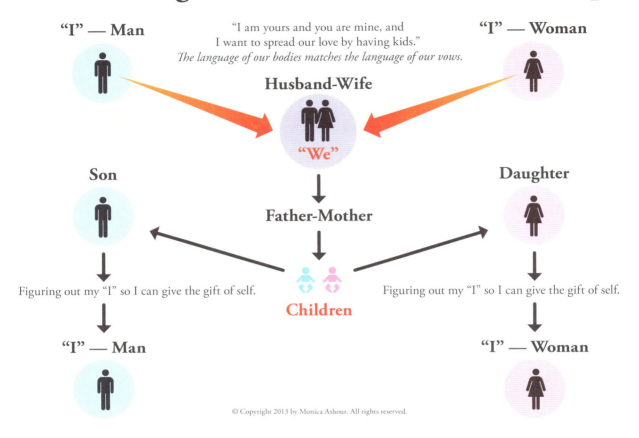

This diagram gives you a good snapshot of the *full vision* of marriage. Only two distinct "I's"—persons who have a good sense of themselves and a good sense of marriage including its openness to children—can enter into marriage in true *freedom*. With a solid sense of self, the two persons are *free* to give themselves *fully* to become a "We."

For instance, when Joe married my sister Katy, they became Joe-*for*-Katy and Katy-*for*-Joe. Through thick and thin, they gave themselves *fully*. Whether they were playing softball, cooking, praying, or watching movies—they were living *for* each other. When their children had hardships, they stuck it out—with and *for* each other and *for* their kids. Through financial security and through financial trouble, they remained *for* each other. And even when Joe developed a debilitating disease, Katy picked up the slack, getting a job, caring *for* him, being *for* him, as she stood by his side until his tragic death. They *fully* gave and *fully* received, reciprocally, throughout their entire marriage. What security the *full* gift of self gives to couples!

"Sexuality, in which man's belonging to the bodily and biological world is expressed, becomes personal and truly human when it is integrated into the relationship of one person to another, in the complete and lifelong mutual gift of a man and a woman." *CCC* 2337

Seven Levels of Intimacy

- Clichés
- Facts
- Opinions
- Hopes and Dreams
- Feelings
- Faults, Fears and Failures
- Legitimate Needs

"GROOM: 'You are an enclosed garden, my sister, my bride, an enclosed garden….'

BRIDE: 'Let my lover come to his garden and eat its choice fruits…I heard my lover knocking'

GROOM: 'Open to me, my sister, my bride….'

BRIDE: '…My heart trembled within me and I grew faint when he spoke….'"

Song of Songs 4:12, 16; 5:2,4

Based on Matthew Kelly's book *Seven Levels of Intimacy*, published by Simon and Schuster. © Copyright 2014 by Monica Ashour. All rights reserved.

Overall, nurturing intimacy on all of these levels ought help us to be "the-best-version-of-ourselves."

ASPECTS OF INTIMACY AT THE LEVEL OF LEGITIMATE NEEDS

Physical
Proper touch from others. Married couples ought to practice tender affirming touch, which includes, but is not limited to sexual touch.

Emotional
Each is in need of and deserves to be heard, accepted, received, and affirmed as he or she is, as a gift.

Intellectual
Being challenged to think. Intellectual stimulation is needed by some immensely, not so much for others.

Spiritual
Loving God above all. The subtlest of needs… usually silence and solitude. Time to be reminded of God's love for us. Recharged relationship.

Part of becoming a "we" entails sharing in a vulnerable way various aspects of life with another. *Intimacy* literally means "to make us known." We all long to know and to be known, our deepest desire, as St. Augustine said, and sharing deeply allows for "into-me-u-see"—intimacy. Such sharing is based on trust, trust that the deepest experiences, feelings, and needs that we reveal will be honored and respected—that "I will be *fully* accepted"—and that "you will be *fully* present to me."

1. Describe a time when you shared with a friend or family member something intimate and you were comforted? What about a time when you shared something very personal but you were not listened to?

2. What experience can you point to that shows that your future spouse accepts you when you shared something intimate? Was it full acceptance? What about when you fully accepted your future spouse's intimate thoughts?

3. What strikes you about this Intimacy Circle? At what level do you and your future spouse tend to share? How can you work fully to listen and risk sharing in a vulnerable way?

Gary Chapman's Five Love Languages

Since love is central to marriage, it is important to know your own and your future spouse's "Love Language." Gary Chapman speaks of 5 Love Languages in his book, *The Five Love Languages: How to Express Heartfelt Commitment to Your Mate.* He says that a "love language" is the way that a person is best able to both **give** and **receive** love.

The following are his five love languages:

Gifts
Actual presents bought or made and given to the other.

Quality Time
Setting aside periods of time to just be together and enjoy each other's presence.

Words of Affirmation
"You really worked hard on that project, and it looks great!" "You look really beautiful!"

Acts of Service
She'd rather have help with the dishes than a bouquet of flowers.
Complimenting him is not as important as preparing lunch.

Physical Touch
Not just sexual contact, but small gestures like hugging and holding hands.

Based on Gary Chapman's book, *The Five Love Languages: How to Express Heartfelt Commitment to Your Mate.* © Copyright 2014 by Monica Ashour. All rights reserved.

"…Love one another with mutual affection; anticipate one another in showing honor."
Romans 12:10

1. What are your top two "love languages"?

2. What are your soon-to-be spouse's top two "love languages"?

3. What were the "love languages" of your mom and your dad? Your future spouse's mom and dad? How might those impact your future marriage?

"Do not live entirely isolated, having retreated into yourselves... but gather instead to seek the common good together."   CCC 1905

Family of Origin: The Good, The Bad, The Ugly

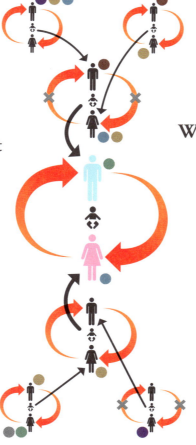

Your Future Family!

Making the most of what you have received requires a total commitment from both of you — to love wounded relatives, to stop the cycle, and to bring healing now and for generations to come.

Also, appreciate and pass on the gifts you have received from your family, such as sense of humor, communication skills, deep faith life, etc.

What Issues Do You Face?
- Addiction
- Abuse
- Codependency
- Depression
- Alcoholism
- Debt
- Mental Illness
- ✕ Divorce

© Copyright 2014 by Monica Ashour. All rights reserved.

What a great gift families are—they are safe havens, places of security, spaces for love and laughter. We know, though, that despite the good times, our families are fallen and as a result, we are fallen. Without judgment, we can take a look at our past and see the good we want to keep and the negative we want to avoid so as to build a healthier family.

1. We suggest you both do a genogram, similar to the example above. Consider the following: What did you discover that you did not already know—about your own family of origin or about your future spouse's family? What are your families' unique gifts? What are the darker areas? How will one's family of origin affect your future marriage?

2. We need not remain "stuck" in a familial pattern, just because that was how we were raised. As you journey toward marriage, discuss with each other what you want to keep or do away with from your family of origin. What cycle needs to be broken, and how will you break it? Are there concerns you have about your or your future spouse's familial, cyclical patterns?

*"Do not judge, and you will not be judged.
Do not condemn, and you will not be condemned.
Forgive, and you will be forgiven."*

Luke 6:37

Replace Fighting with Safe Dialogue

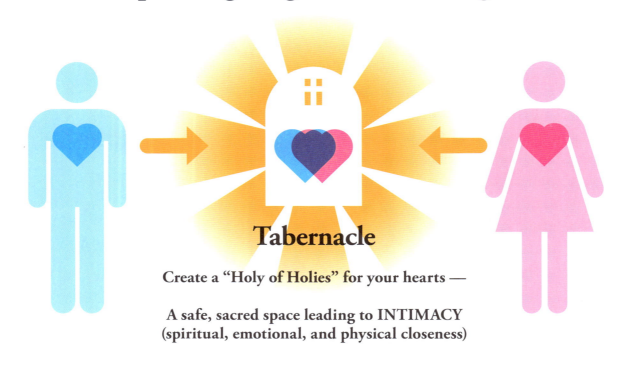

How to Have a Safe Dialogue

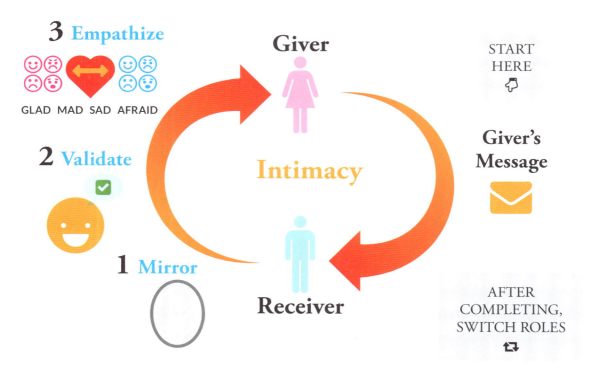

How to Have a Safe Dialogue: An Example

 Giver's Message: *"You're usually late — that hurts my feelings."*

Receiver's Response:

1 Mirror

I'm often late and that hurts your feelings. Did I get that right? Yes.

Is there more? Yes, I feel hurt because it seems you don't love me.

You feel hurt because it seems I don't love you. Did I get that right? Yes.

Is there more? No.

2 Validate

It makes sense that you feel hurt and unloved when I'm late.

3 Empathize

I can imagine you feel *mad*.

Actually, I'm *afraid*… Oh, I can see that now.

AFTER COMPLETING, SWITCH ROLES

Based on *A New Way to Love: A Guide for Catholic Couples* by Harville Hendrix, Ph.D. and Helen LaKelly Hunt, Ph.D., with Drs. Kathryn and Ron Rombs.
© Copyright 2015 by Monica Ashour. All rights reserved.

Giver (Husband): I was late; I'm so sorry. I have been trying to get a raise at work so that we can go on that vacation and so the kids can play sports and take tap. The whole time that I was delayed, you were on my mind. I'm sorry you feel scared. I love you.

Receiver (Wife) (Mirror): If I got you right, you are sorry you were late, but you are trying to get a raise at work…. I've been on your mind the whole time. You are sorry that I feel scared. And you love me. Did I get that right?

Giver: Yes.

Receiver: Is there more?

Giver: Yes. I also worked longer to surprise you with a two-day get-a-way weekend while we hire a babysitter.

Receiver (Mirror): If I got you right, you worked longer to surprise me with a two-day get-a-way weekend while we hire a babysitter, right?

Giver: Right.

Receiver: Is there more?

Giver: No.

Receiver (Validate): It makes sense that you want to stay late to get enough money so that we can enjoy a vacation together.

Receiver (Empathize): I can imagine you feel mad that you are working extra for the family and you feel unappreciated. Is that right? Do you feel mad at me?

Giver: Actually, no. I feel scared. I'm afraid I do more and more for you but that is not enough.

Receiver: If I got you right, you feel scared, not mad, that you do so much for me but that is not enough. Right?

Giver: Right.

Receiver: I am so sorry that you feel scared. I appreciate all you do for me and our family. I love you.

(Full, two-minute, silent hug)

Breakthrough: The wounds of fear of inadequacy and abandonment are resolved, and safety returns. Safety and intimacy are linked. Rather than both feeling isolated, now they both are filled with the "wedding feeling" of wonder, reverence, and love.

In order for your two "I's" to come together and become a "We," you need a "sacred, safe space" where you can be assured of authentic communication. You need to be able to trust each other not to attack. Without trust being established, it is very difficult to be intimate. When you encounter a challenge, agree to take a step away from it. Then, enter into the "Tabernacle" of your mutual love, and be present to each other. Mirroring, validating, and empathizing are ways to show your beloved that you can be entrusted with his/her full, vulnerable gift of self.

1. Can you trust your fiancée/fiancé so that you can be vulnerably intimate with him or her? Why or why not?

2. Why is empathy so important in relationships? Share a time when you felt empathy for your beloved or when he/she felt empathy for you.

3. Try a few Safe Dialogues. Possible topics: Which brother or sister is closest to you and why? What are the strengths and weaknesses regarding the way your parents raised you? What are you feeling regarding a potential job change or move?

Communication Breakdown

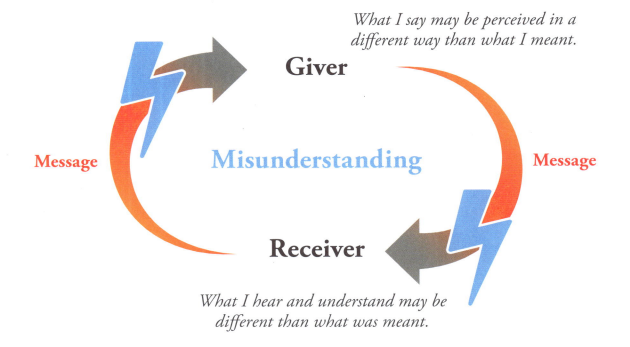

Communication Breakdown: HALT!

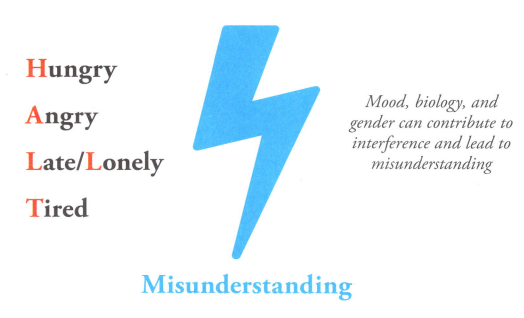

Reacting from Core Wounds Causes Marital Conflict
Husband's Main Fear: Am I Man Enough?

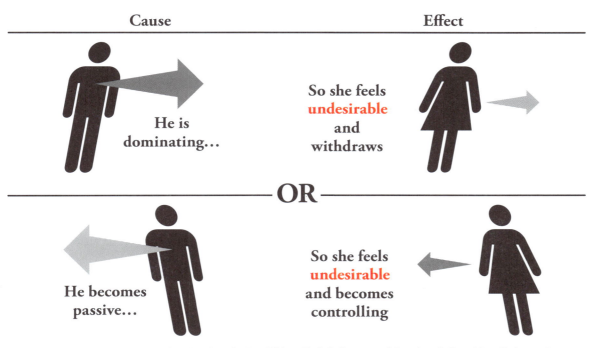

Reacting from Core Wounds Causes Marital Conflict
Wife's Main Fear: Am I Desirable?

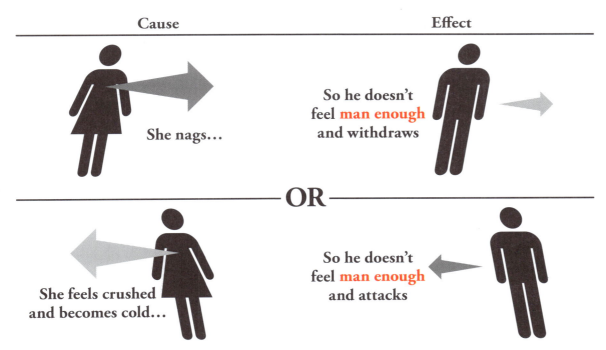

Tilted Relationship

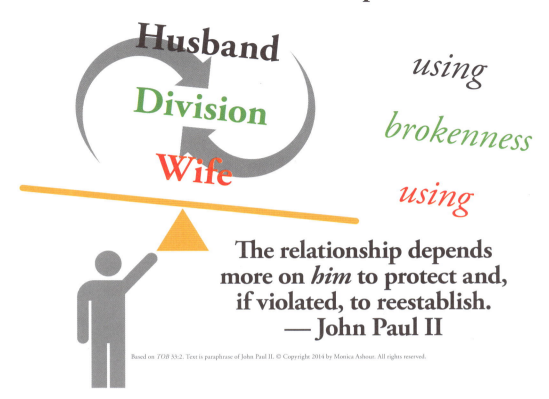

AFTER THE FALL:

"Your urge shall be for your husband and he will dominate over you."

Genesis 3:16

Husband

Division

Wife

using

brokenness

using

The relationship depends more on *him* to protect and, if violated, to reestablish.
— John Paul II

Based on *TOB* 33:2. Text is paraphrase of John Paul II. © Copyright 2014 by Monica Ashour. All rights reserved.

Balanced Reciprocity

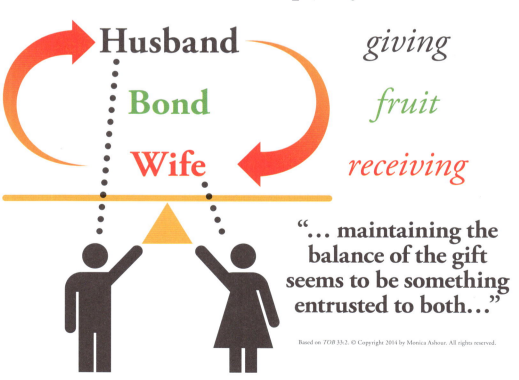

AFTER REDEMPTION:

"Behold, I make all things new."

Revelations 21:5

Husband

Bond

Wife

giving

fruit

receiving

"… maintaining the balance of the gift seems to be something entrusted to both…"

Based on *TOB* 33:2. © Copyright 2014 by Monica Ashour. All rights reserved.

Red Flags of Domestic Violence

Emotional
Constant criticism, namecalling, profanity, manipulation as a norm, addictions to alcohol, porn, drugs.

Psychological
Intimidation, threats, neglect, isolating victim from family and friends, unreasonable demands, constantly controlling victim's schedule, making victim feel crazy or guilty, the silent treatment, deliberately doing things that the victim despises.

Financial
Limiting victim's access to funds, preventing or demanding victim to work, withdrawing huge amounts of money or making large purchases that victim would not approve of, making all financial decisions when the victim wants a say.

Sexual
Any sexual act forced upon victim, sharing intimate details in public, manipulating through sex— withholding or making demands, lust.

Physical
Violent acts such as hitting, kicking, biting, and pushing. Objects thrown, destruction of property, reckless risks with potential endangerment.

Healthy Conflicts

Irritation, wishing he/she understood more, misunderstandings, frailties

Fights, but conversations later to reconcile

Disagreement about debts or purchases, mutual compromise

Frustration but understanding hormonal differences, "use" if present should fade

Release of anger and disappointment in appropriate ways

Advice from a TOBET member who, at age 26, left an abusive marriage: "Before you decide to marry, notice even the smallest red flag, for it will escalate after marriage exponentially. Ask the opinion of an unbiased counselor privately. I wish I had."

Based on *For Your Marriage* at www.USCCB.org. **Domestic Hotline 1-800–799–SAFE (7233).** "No person is expected to stay in an abusive marriage." — U.S. Bishops. © Copyright 2014 by Monica Ashour. All rights reserved.

2 FULL

HEALTHY CONFLICT RESOLUTION: *Advice from Experts*

Help your relationship by being the first to step outside the comfort zone.

Use the Generosity Gauge, rather than the Fairness Filter.

Authors
Jennifer Roback Morse & Betsy Kerekes
101 Tips for a Happier Marriage
www.ruthinstitute.org

The second section in his book describes disenchantment, frustration, and anger. He also addresses jealousy, relationships with other family members, balancing work with marriage, and managing money.

Author and psychotherapist
Peter M. Kalellis, Ph.D.
Living in Difficult Relationships
www.peterkalellis.com

Get rid of "Negativity" ("any transaction that the other experiences as hurtful") by tracking "Zero Negativity" days, resulting in healing and renewal.

Use Safe Conversation exercise so as to "discover the other and experience connection." (See earlier diagrams.)

Authors and psychotherapists
Harville Hendrix, Ph. D. & Helen LaKelly Hunt, Ph.D.
"A New Way to Love: A Guide for Catholic Couples."
www.couplehoodstore.com/catholic

Communication:
clear vs. vague;
open vs. guarded;
honest vs. dishonest;
effective vs. ineffective;
effective communication is responsive to the other's needs with true feelings shared and needs being stated clearly.

Author and psychotherapist
John Farrelly
The Good Marriage Guide
www.veritasbooksonline.com/ authors/f/j/john-farrelly.html

TOBET4ENGAGED   29

Battle of the Sexes

Man **vs.** Woman	Man **and** Woman
Everyone for himself/herself	For ourselves, the world, the Church and God
Misery of detachment	Joy of reciprocal giving and receiving
Bodies are tools for use	Bodies are gifts for love
Division and isolation	Working toward a better world
"Divide and conquer"	*Communion of Persons*

"[All of history is determined by...] who she will be for him and he for her."
TOB **43:7**

Based on *TOB* 28:3, 32:3 and 43:7. © Copyright 2014 by Monica Ashour. All rights reserved.

For the past several pages, we have had to face the reality that relationships are messy. Issues will come up that need serious reflection, but if you are *fully* committed to each other, then you will find solutions to these issues. When you both know that you are *for* the other, through thick and thin, then conflicts do not need to be scary—you need not be afraid.

Forgiveness is the key. It is no accident that Jesus says to forgive 70 times 7 times—a large number, implying over and over and over again! Working through conflict is an essential task of marriage. Thinking that marriage is going to be easy is not taking seriously that becoming a "we" takes time and practice and humility and reverence and love. You might remember that none of us *deserves* forgiveness from Jesus; it is a sheer, undeserving gift of mercy. In the same way that we receive this gift from God, we should offer it to our future spouse. Embrace the cross of sacrificial, forgiving love—for yourself and for your future spouse.

1. Share with each other a time in your distant past when you experienced unexpected forgiveness.

2. Which elements of HALT are you most susceptible to: Hungry, Angry, Lonely/Late, or Tired? What about for your future spouse?

3. Men: Do you experience the core fear of "Am I Man Enough/Am I Capable?" If not, what is your core fear? How will you work to act out of a place of healing rather than woundedness in your future marriage?

4. Women: Do you experience the core fear of "Am I Desirable?" If not, what is your core fear? How will you work to act out of a place of healing rather than woundedness in your future marriage?

5. What are some specific ways to know that your future spouse is a person willing to extend forgiveness, as well as being a person willing to ask for forgiveness?

Dave Ramsey's Financial Peace University

Put It All on the Table	**Transparency is the key!**
"Marry" Your Accounts	**When you get married, combining your money into joint accounts is a crucial step.**
Start Budgeting Together	**Put your combined income and expenses on paper, on purpose, and determine what a typical month is going to look like.**
Make A Plan	**Once everything is on the table, determine what 'Baby Step' you are on—as a couple!**
Put Your Relationship First	**Whatever you do, don't stress! It's just money.**

Financial Peace University (FPU) is Dave Ramsey's program with classes offered at locations all over the nation. Learn more about this life-changing class at www.daveramsey.com and locate one in your area to attend as you prepare for marriage. © Copyright 2014 by Monica Ashour. All rights reserved.

Dave Ramsey's Seven Baby Steps to Financial Peace

Baby Step 1	**$1,000 Emergency Fund**
Baby Step 2	**Pay off all debt using the Debt Snowball**
Baby Step 3	**3 to 6 months of expenses in savings**
Baby Step 4	**Invest 15% in Roth IRAs and pre-tax retirement**
Baby Step 5	**College funding for children**
Baby Step 6	**Pay off your house early**
Baby Step 7	**Build wealth and give! (See Ramsey on Tithing)**

Financial Peace University (FPU) is Dave Ramsey's program with classes offered at locations all over the nation. Learn more about this life-changing class at www.daveramsey.com and locate one in your area to attend as you prepare for marriage. © Copyright 2014 by Monica Ashour. All rights reserved.

TOBET4ENGAGED

FICO® Credit Score Chart

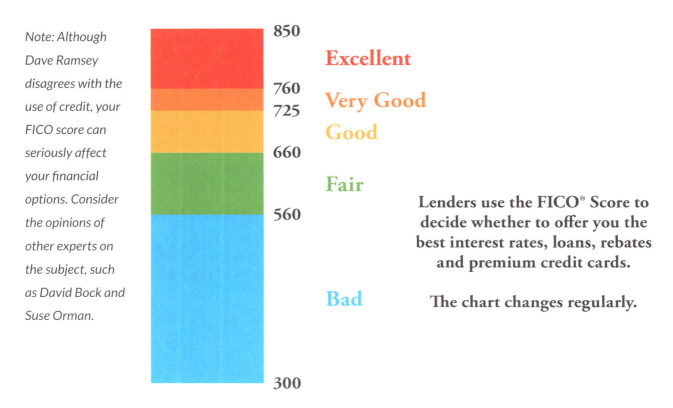

Note: Although Dave Ramsey disagrees with the use of credit, your FICO score can seriously affect your financial options. Consider the opinions of other experts on the subject, such as David Bock and Suse Orman.

850 — Excellent
760 — Very Good
725 — Good
660 — Fair
560 — Bad
300

Lenders use the FICO® Score to decide whether to offer you the best interest rates, loans, rebates and premium credit cards.

The chart changes regularly.

Based on a chart from 2011 by SmartMoneyTalk.com. © Copyright 2014 by Monica Ashour. All rights reserved.

Danger Zone: Lending Money

57% of people surveyed said they have seen a friendship or relationship ruined because one person didn't pay back the other.

50% have loaned $100 or more to help someone

55% of these are not repaid

50%

If you help with money, make it a GIFT instead of a LOAN— keep your relationships strong.

Based on Dave Ramsey's Financial Peace University. © Copyright 2014 by Monica Ashour. All rights reserved.

Dave Ramsey on Tithing

"We make a living by what we get, but we make a life by what we give."

What?	To 'tithe' means to give 10% of gross revenue.
Benefits?	Tithing was created for **our benefit.** It is to teach us how to keep God first in our lives and how to be unselfish people. Unselfish people make better husbands, wives, friends, relatives, employees and employers. God is trying to teach us how to prosper over time. Our giving helps **those in need.**
Who says?	"A tithe of everything belongs to the LORD…" Lev 27:30–33. **Jesus** said, "This poor widow has put in more than all of them, for all of them contributed out of their abundance, but she out of her poverty." Lk 21:1–4
Really?	If you cannot live off 90% of your income, then you cannot live off 100%.
Why?	Read the Bible and take from it what you will, and if you tithe, do it out of **love for God,** not guilt.
When?	Always. The Bible does not mention anything about 'pausing' tithing [in financial distress].
BONUS	**Take the tax deduction!**

"Giving liberates the soul of the giver."

Financial Peace University (FPU) is Dave Ramsey's program with classes offered at locations all over the nation. Learn more about this life-changing class at www.daveramsey.com and locate one in your area to attend as you prepare for marriage. © Copyright 2014 by Monica Ashour. All rights reserved.

"Truly I tell you, whatever you did for one of the least of these brothers and sisters of mine, you did for me."

Matthew 25:40

1. Why do you think money is such a sensitive topic with couples? Why is it a source of tension, even leading to divorce?

2. A happily married man of 35 years said, "Money is not the deeper issue. It is what money represents: security. If a couple can communicate, really communicate about money, it will not be a deal breaker." Do you agree? Why or why not?

3. Are you willing to change the way you approach/think about money? What if your soon-to-be spouse won't change? What can you do about it?

4. Which are you and which is your future spouse: Tightwad or Spendthrift or Moderate? How will that reality affect your marriage?

5. Do you see money as a gift from God and not only yours? Have you discussed tithing to your parish? Do you give to charities that promote the dignity of the person—to which will you give? Tithing is also giving 10% of your time and talent. How will you actively tithe to your church/community?
   (Note: This can mean living the Corporal and Spiritual Works of Mercy. See *CCC* 2447.)

6. You may want to spend time to seek guidance and dialogue about the following:

   Life and Disability Insurance
   Credit Score/Repair and a Retirement Plan
   Creating a will including guardianship
   of children should you both die

Catholic Finance Guy: Thomas E. Zordani, tom@faithfinances.net, www.faithfinances.net

All Christians Believe…

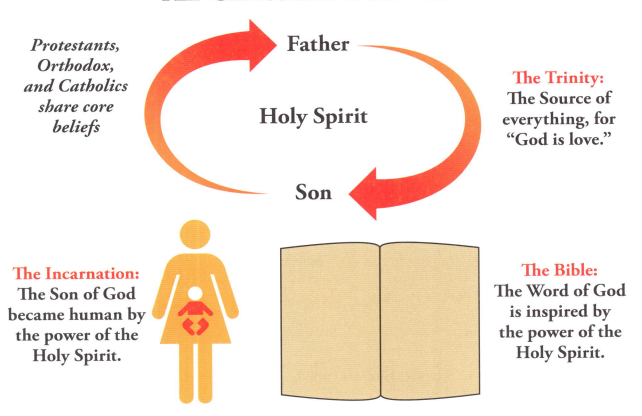

Protestants, Orthodox, and Catholics share core beliefs

The Trinity: The Source of everything, for "God is love."

The Incarnation: The Son of God became human by the power of the Holy Spirit.

The Bible: The Word of God is inspired by the power of the Holy Spirit.

© Copyright 2014 by Monica Ashour. All rights reserved.

So far in this section on giving the *full* gift of self to form a "we," we have covered intimate sharing and communication, sources of division and forgiveness, and finances—all of which can either bring you closer as a couple or be barriers to union. Now it is time to cover another area of central importance: *religion*. The word *religion* means "to bind together again," as in a community bonded together by faith.

Those of you who come from different religious traditions such as Judaism or Hinduism can still agree on principles that unite all humans: treating every person with dignity, respecting the beliefs of the other, realizing that love is integral in any good relationship. One of my closest Catholic friends married an atheist who always supports her in her faith life. Knowing their children are going to be raised in the Catholic Church, he goes to Mass with her.

For those who are Christians—Orthodox, Protestant, or Catholic—you are united in believing that Jesus Christ is the Son of God who saves us, that He is revealed to us in the Incarnation and in Scripture, and that the Blessed Trinity is the foundation of all, because "God is Love."

Nevertheless, being a practicing Catholic entails going to Mass every Sunday, not as a mere obligation, but to worship God in a communal way and to be strengthened by the very Body and Blood of Jesus, which is not a symbol but reality. Be serious in your discussion of divisions, while convinced in your commonalities.

1. What does faith mean to you and why? What does the Bible mean to you and why?

2. How can you encourage your future spouse in his or her spiritual journey?

3. How significant is your religion to you? To your future spouse? If there are differences, how can your relationship be strengthened rather than harmed by such differences?

4. For those of differing faiths, how are you going to handle the issue of religion, especially when it comes to raising children?

*"You were called to freedom…
only do not use your freedom as a pretext to indulge
the flesh, but through love, serve one another."*

Galatians 5:13

Approaches to the Church and Freedom

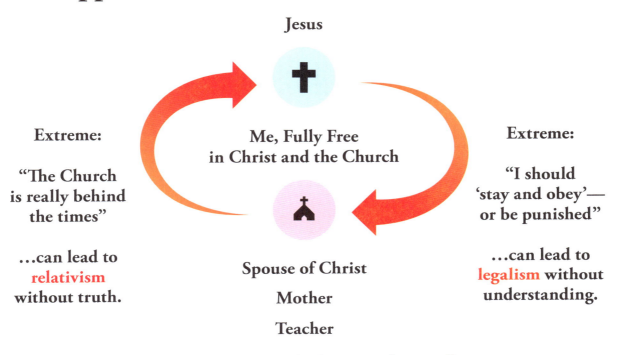

*I am truly free and fully human when I submit
to God's law of love, entrusted to the Church.*

© Copyright 2014 by Monica Ashour. All rights reserved.

One of my friends, a religious sister who wears a full-length, white habit, tells of a delightful encounter: "One day, when I was grocery shopping, I noticed a little girl staring at me. I smiled warmly. Then, very loudly, the little girl said to her mom, 'Mama! She's getting married!'"

Out of the mouths of babes! The religious sister represents all of us, the Body-Bride of Christ—the Church. So often people hear the word *church* and have a negative reaction, but Christ Himself loves the Church, entrusting Himself *fully* to his Body-Bride the Church. The Church, in turn, guides us to love. Every single teaching of the Church is given to us in order to safeguard love.

1. How would you describe the Church? How would your future spouse describe the Church?

2. What are your insights into Christianity? What do you think about secularism's growing force against religious freedom?

"Man's dignity therefore requires him to act out of conscious and free choice, as moved and drawn in a personal way from within, and not by blind impulses in himself or by mere external constraint. Man gains such dignity when, ridding himself of all slavery to the passions, he presses forward to his goal by freely choosing what is good, and by his diligence and skill, effectively secures for himself the means suited to this end."

Gaudium et Spes 17

Marriage Statistics

Percent of Couples Married for Life

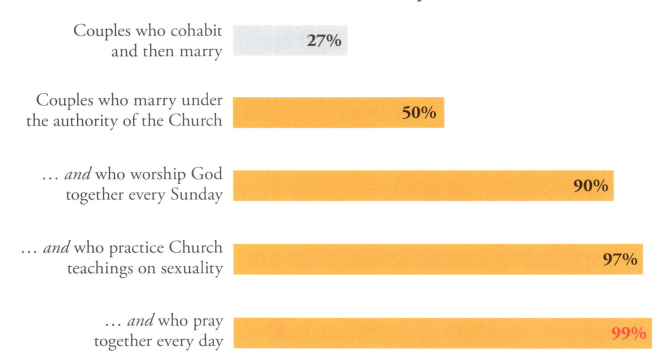

Based on Tommy Nelson's statistics in *The Book of Romance*. © Copyright 2014 by Monica Ashour. All rights reserved.

"Tobiah arose from bed and said to his wife, 'My love, get up. Let us pray and beg our Lord to have mercy on us and to grant us deliverance.' She got up, and they started to pray…
'Lord, you know that I take this wife of mine not because of lust but for a noble purpose. Call down your mercy on me and on her, and allow us to live together to a happy old age.'"

Tobit 8:4-5, 7-8

In previous generations, dating and engaged couples did not live together. It was expected that committed love was to be professed publicly at a wedding before the couple lived together.

Now, it seems that pragmatism and financial expedience, rather than real commitment, dictate couples' decisions. Cohabitation allows for an easy way out of a relationship. It seems to feed directly into the deepest insecurities of a man—"Am I man enough"—and into the deepest insecurities of a woman—"Am I desirable?" The statistics speak for themselves.

1. Why do you think cohabitation is so prominent nowadays? Do you think this helps society and relationships?
2. Why do you think only 27% of couples who lived together before marriage stay married?
3. You may be living together now. What steps can you take to prepare for a true, lifelong marriage?
4. How can we align our engagement with God's law of love?

FOR MORE COHABITATION STATISTICS AND INFORMATION:
nationalmarriageproject.org/wp-content/uploads/2013/01/ShouldWeLiveTogether.pdf
www.citizenlink.com/2010/06/14/does-cohabitation-protect-against-divorce/

"Father, that they may be one as you and I are one."

John 17:21

Pathways to Marital Communion

Area	Obstacles	Communication
Spiritual unity	Apathy and spiritual warfare	Praying and worshipping
Emotional intimacy	Wounds and isolation	Listening and expressing
Teamwork	Selfishness and control	Mutual submission
Reconciling	Pride and bitterness	Apologizing and forgiving
Sexual intimacy	Lust and insensitivity	Affection and love-making

By Dr. Bob Schuchts of The John Paul II Healing Center, Tallahassee, Florida. Used by permission. © Copyright 2013 by Monica Ashour. All rights reserved.

"And be kind to one another, compassionate, forgiving one another as God has forgiven you in Christ."

Ephesians 4:32

We conclude this section of our guide with the Pathways to Marital Communion. Awareness of obstacles and the measures to counter these obstacles are a big step toward staying married.

One final reality worth mentioning that Pope Francis often speaks about is the devil. Lucifer is a fallen angel who wants to divide people from God and from each other. The great Christian writer, C.S. Lewis, says that the best trick of the devil is for him to convince us that he does not exist.

Be not afraid, however, for Jesus is much more powerful than the Evil One. Our Lord's love is free, full, faithful, and fruitful and is always available to you, so that you can, in turn, love each other freely, fully, faithfully, and fruitfully. These are the 4 Fs that can really never be divided, for true love is whole.

1. Which of the obstacles strikes you most and why?

2. Which do you think is the area you two will need the most work to overcome?

POTENTIAL "BATTLEGROUND" ISSUES

1. **Where do I plan on spending holidays?**
   a. At my parents' house.
   b. At your parents' house.
   c. At our house.
   d. Both my and your parents' house. (Divided Time)

2. **When we have children:**
   a. I will work and provide.
   b. I will stay home and raise the children.
   c. We will both work to provide and have daycare/ nanny/family for our children.
   d. We are not open to the gift of children.

3. **When we get married, our money will be...**
   a. placed in one joint account.
   b. kept in separate accounts but we both have access.
   c. kept in separate accounts; I keep what I make and you keep what you make.
   d. kept in some other way. Explain.

4. **When we get married, we will practice our faith by:**
   a. both going to the church *we* attend together.
   b. both of us going to *my* church together every Sunday.
   c. both of us going to *your* church together every Sunday.
   d. alternating Sundays at two different churches.
   e. doing our own thing (one or both of us will not attend church).

5. **Whenever we have difficult feelings about each other or face a conflict, I prefer to:**
   a. remain silent.
   b. say something as soon as the difficult feelings arise.
   c. wait a certain amount of time before raising the issue.
   d. do something else. If so, what?

6. **I should use credit cards:**
   a. when I find a good sale on something I have wanted but don't have funds.
   b. for everything I can to earn points/flyer miles but then pay them off each month to avoid interest.
   c. in emergency situations only.
   d. when I need to cover expenses at the end of the month when my paycheck is falling short of covering my purchases.
   e. never. We should never use credit cards.

7. **If we find ourselves in a difficult situation financially, I am likely to:**
   a. ask my parents for help.
   b. ask your parents for help.
   c. put it on a credit card or take out a loan.
   d. get a second job, sell something.

8. **How would you rate these priorities in your life (with 1 being most important):**
   __ Work   __ School/learning
   __ Extended family   __ Children
   __ Spouse   __ Friends
   __ Church   __ Pets
   __ Hobbies / Recreation

9. **When it comes to our relationship, who should know about what our struggles are:**
   a. it should stay between us.
   b. close family and/or friends.
   c. I vent on Facebook or tweet what I am thinking and feeling.
   d. it should stay between us and our therapist or pastor.

10. **How do you manage time?**
    a. I think schedules are "suggestions."
    b. I am very time conscious and I try to be early.
    c. I try to be on time but I rather look my best and be there fashionably late.
    d. I like to get there late and maybe even leave early.

11. **True** or **False**   We will try to make a budget and work/sacrifice to live within those financial guidelines.

12. **True** or **False**   Taking a vacation every year is an expectation I have for our future.

13. **True** or **False**   I think the use of pornography is normal and healthy.

14. **True** or **False**   I would think less of my spouse or become annoyed if they passed gas in front of me even if they excused themselves.

15. How much money should I be allowed to spend before discussing it first with my spouse? (Write out below.)

    $ _____

PART 3

The Gift of Love is FAITHFUL

"WE" LIVING THE SACRAMENTALITY OF MARRIAGE & THE MEANING OF SEX

The Four F's

Love is… giving
Love is… receiving

Free
"I lay my life down freely." Jn 10:18
"May it be done unto me according to your word." Lk 1:38

Full
"This is my body, given." Lk 22:19
"[Mary was] standing by the Cross of Jesus." Jn 19:25

Faithful
"I will be with you until the end of time." Mt 28:20
"Do whatever He tells you." Jn 2:5

Fruitful
"[The Father] will give you the Advocate." Jn 14:16
"Woman, behold your son; [John], behold your mother." Jn 19:26-27

Based on *Humanae Vitae*. © Copyright 2014 by Monica Ashour. All rights reserved.

Now we move from discussing a *free* "I" capable of giving a *full* gift (in order to form a "we") to a vow of permanence: "I am yours and you are mine," *faithfully*. The example of Jesus and Mary—a *faithful* man and a *faithful* woman—paves the way for understanding and living securely in love.

1. Have you ever thought of love as *receiving* in addition to *giving*? What difference does that make in your future marriage?

2. In loving your future spouse, which of the Four F's is the easiest to live out? Which is the most difficult? Which are easiest and most difficult for your future spouse in loving you? How will that impact your marriage?

"Thus the marriage bond has been established by God himself in such a way that a marriage concluded and consummated between baptized persons can never be dissolved. This bond, which results from the free human acts of the spouses and their consummation of the marriage, is a reality, henceforth irrevocable, and gives rise to a covenant guaranteed by God's fidelity. The Church does not have the power to contravene this disposition of divine wisdom." CCC 1640

Sacramental Vision of Baptism

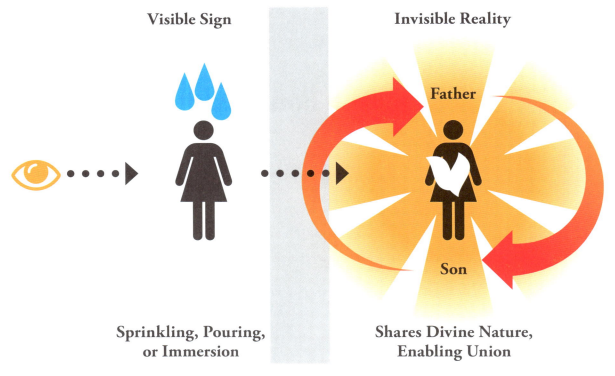

Sacramental Vision of Marriage

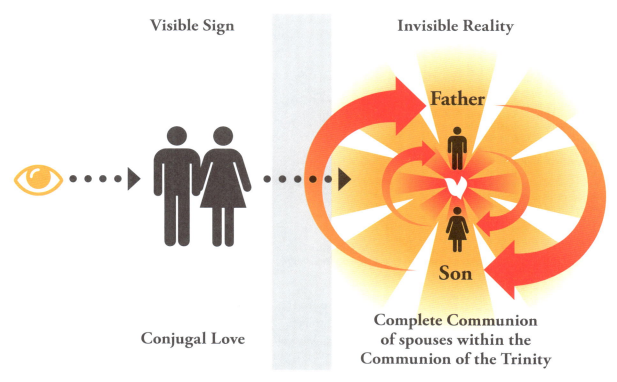

Sacraments of Baptism and Matrimony

Sacrament	Visible Sign	Invisible Reality
Baptism	*Language of Words* "I baptize you in the **Name of the Father, the Son and the Holy Spirit**"	Given a share in the **name and nature** of God and become members of **His family**
	Language of the Body Water is **sprinkled** or **poured** (or you are **immersed and brought up**)	**Washed** from original sin and **'drowned'** into Jesus' death so we can **rise** with Him in divine life
Matrimony	*Language of Words* Man and woman **exchange vows:** Free, full, faithful and fruitful	Each **freely consents** to enter into marriage and to live for the other: Free, full, faithful and fruitful
	Language of the Body Male body and female body come together in a **one-flesh union** that is free, full, faithful, and fruitful.	**Two persons become united indissolubly** reflecting the bond of Jesus and the Church that is free, full, faithful, and fruitful.

© Copyright 2014 by Monica Ashour. All rights reserved.

In order to understand the sacrament you are about to give to and receive from each other (remember: *you*, not the minister, priest, or deacon, are the official ministers of the sacrament), let's remind ourselves what a sacrament is.

Earlier, we defined the Sacramental View of Reality—that the visible *reveals* and *brings about* the invisible. For example, at baptism, we see the visible reality of water being poured, which indicates or reveals a *cleansing*. That is precisely what happens: We were *cleansed* from original sin and partake in divine life through Jesus' gift of self on the Cross, a gift that is so *faithful* that it transcends time and space, allowing us to be in Communion with God. This gift from Jesus is permanent—*faithful*—He will never ever take back his offer of love. You received Jesus' gift of self at your baptism and are to continue to say "Yes" to God, who strengthens you to say "Yes" to each other.

In the Sacrament of Matrimony, the outward sign is the coming together in sexual intercourse of the two spouses, whose distinct bodies allow for union. This "one-flesh union," spoken about by Jesus in Scripture (Matthew 19, referring to Genesis 2:24), reveals and brings about a unity that is *indissoluble*—in other words, *faithful*, never-to-be-erased, forever, "there's no way out!" St. John Paul speaks about this one-flesh union as revealing the two becoming like *one organism*—you and your future spouse living life together in mutual fidelity, never to be dissected or split from each other. What security faithfulness brings!

Marriage, like baptism, brings God's life to bear on the earth. Conjugal love that is free, full, faithful, and fruitful is a way of saying to God with your bodies, "We invite you, Lord, to be the center of our relationship, for we long to be *faithful* to each other, but we need your help."

1. What strikes you about the Sacramental Vision of Marriage? Why would God make sex so profound?

2. Without water, baptism is impossible.
   Without sex, marriage is impossible.
   How does such a reality show the sacredness of sex, given the proper context of marriage?

3. Baptism is our *yes* to union with Jesus. Marriage is two people's *yes* to union with each other in Jesus. How can this parallel help you understand and enter into your future marriage more deeply?

TOBET4ENGAGED   41

A Comparison—
The Eucharist and Marriage

	Language of Words	Language of the Body
 "This is my Body, given"	Consent: "Amen" (Renewal of Baptismal Vow)	Body-to-Body Union of Christ, the Groom and His Church, the Bride

"Full, conscious, and active participation at Mass"* yields fruitfulness of daily sacrifice for all of God's family

 "This is my body, given"	Consent: Four F's (Renewal of Marriage Vows)	Body-to-body Consummation of Husband and Wife

Full, conscious, and active participation in family life yields fruitfulness of daily sacrifice for your family

Based on *CCC* 1638-41, 2427; *TOB* 131 and *Constitution on the Sacred Liturgy*, 11. © Copyright 2014 by Monica Ashour. All rights reserved.

Sacrament of Matrimony

Language of Words:
Spoken Vows with "Four F's"
Free, Full, Faithful, Fruitful

Language of the Body:
Conjugal Intercourse with "Four F's"
Free, Full, Faithful, Fruitful

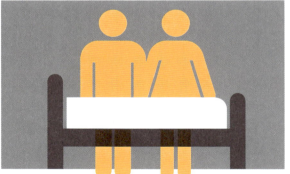

"The sacramental word is… only a sign of the coming to be of marriage."

"Without this consummation, marriage is not yet constituted in its full reality."

From *TOB* 103:2. © Copyright 2015 by Monica Ashour. All rights reserved.

"He who eats My flesh and drinks My blood abides in Me, and I in him." — John 6:56

3 FAITHFUL

42 TOBET4**ENGAGED**

HERE IT IS!

THIS IS WHAT YOU WILL BE SAYING ON YOUR WEDDING DAY... AND WEDDING NIGHT

Language of ...

Words		Body
"Have you come here freely and without reservation...?"	**FREELY**	Free gift of self in conjugal love.
Canon Law 1057, 1058, 1066		
"...to give yourself to each other in marriage?"	**FULLY**	Full gift of self in conjugal love.
Canon Law 1055, 1056		
"Will you love and honor each other as man and wife for the rest of your lives?"	**FAITHFULLY**	Faithful gift of self in conjugal love.
Canon Law 1059, 1060		
"Will you accept children lovingly, and bring them up according to the law of Christ and His Church?"	**FRUITFULLY**	Fruitful gift of self in conjugal love.
Canon Law 1061		

Based on concepts from Dr. Nguyen of the Institute of Pastoral Theology at Ave Maria University. © Copyright 2014 by Monica Ashour. All rights reserved.

What a beautiful moment when you will take vows at the sacred altar before God, family, and friends, where you declare to each other your consent that you will live out the Four F's in all of your married life. Isn't it amazing that the language of your words of consent is so powerful that, then and there, your marriage begins, ratified by the language of your body on your honeymoon?!

There are some who take vows lightly insofar as they say these words before God, the Church, others, and their beloved without really meaning them—they don't intend to live out the Four F's. This is why annulments can be granted. In those situations, the marriage cannot take place because there is a barrier to true commitment at the time of the vows. For instance, a person may not have the first F of Freedom if he or she has an ongoing addiction. Full is lacking if one does not intend to give every aspect of his/her life to the other. Faithful love may be seen by one party or both parties as unnecessary

or irrelevant. And the F of Fruitful is shunned if either party is not open to children.

On page 1 of this book, we mentioned St. John Paul's exhortation that all engaged persons ought to "test" the truth of their love before making formal declarations. In other words, be persons of integrity—do not go through a ceremony that is empty of meaning. Rather, discuss your future vows in an extremely serious way, making sure that you and your fiancé/fiancée are going to enter into the Four F's in truth and love. When vows are made honestly, your marriage is set on a secure foundation of truth and love, with Christ as the center, giving you the foundation for a happy marriage.

1. Do you intend to live out the Four F's? Does your future spouse?

2. Can you make vows at the altar in all honesty as a person of integrity? Can your future spouse?

TOBET4ENGAGED 43

Why Save Sex for the Wedding Night?

Having Sex before Wedding Night	Waiting until Wedding Night for Sex
Rejects God's plan for sex in marriage and shows lack of trust in God	Accepts God's plan for sex in marriage and trusts that God's laws are good for us
Gives in to the sin of fornication — treats wedding night as meaningless	Waits for the joy of consummation — looks with longing to wedding night
Rejects fullness of meaning in wedding vows	Accepts fullness of meaning in wedding vows
Says "I can't wait; I can't say no"	Says "You're worth waiting for"
Creates a precedent for future infidelity to vows	Is an apprenticeship in future fidelity to vows
Tends to stall relationship growth; a partner can feel fearful and vulnerable without vows	Allows for continued growth in intimacy; both can feel safe and securely loved
Dominated by pleasure and self-gratification, the two are enslaved to their feelings of sexual passion	Guided by reverence and self-mastery, the two freely choose to conform to the meaning of sex
Speaks a lie: "You're all mine NOW!"	Tells the truth: "We're not a one-flesh union yet!"
Treats sex as essentially casual	Treats sex as essentially sacramental

St. John Paul II says that proclaiming the truth of the body and sex is not a condemnation, but an *invitation* to a free, full, faithful, and fruitful life.

Created by Steve Patton, M.A., J.D. Used with permission. © Copyright 2015 by Monica Ashour. All rights reserved.

"The two become one flesh." —Genesis 2:24

Some say, "Why doesn't the Church get out of our bedroom! Our sex life is our own. We can do whatever we want with our bodies—it's our choice!" It is true—we can do what we want, but Pope John Paul's theology of the body is his invitation for us to take a look at the truth and meaning of sex and the body so as to experience deep, abiding love.

We said earlier that a smile has its own meaning, as does gazing into each other's eyes. Sex, too, has its own meaning: "I'm married to you, and I'm ready to form a family with you." The Church does not want the most intimate act between two humans to be emptied of its deep meaning, no more than She would want the Eucharist to be emptied of its deep meaning.

The Church's teachings are like a beautiful mosaic. If we begin to disregard a teaching here, a teaching there, one piece at a time, then the entire "artwork" of Christianity's call to love is tarnished. Please be open-minded about this and discuss it seriously with your beloved, for the mosaic is all about love. Sexual integrity also forms a mosaic of your own family life, affecting every aspect.

1. On Friday night—the night before your wedding—sexual intercourse is called fornication, a sin. On Saturday night—the night of your wedding (and thereafter)—sexual intercourse is called consummation, a truthful, loving union which worships God. What makes the difference? Discuss this change.

2. By understanding that the Language of the Body is to match the Language of Words of the Vows, you can reflect sexual honesty and integrity—words and actions and their meaning go together. How can you live now, as well as after you are married, in sexual honesty?

3. Have you ever thought of the Church's teachings being a mosaic? What would it mean for the rest of the Church's teachings if the 4 F's were not necessary in marital intercourse?

"Jesus said in reply…'So they are no longer two, but one flesh. Therefore, what God has joined together, no human being must separate.'"
Matthew 19:4, 6

Conjugal love is not closed in on itself; it is fruitful, beyond the bedroom walls. C.S. Lewis reminds us that marital intercourse is face-to-face, thereby strengthening the couple's friendship, so that they then are equipped to face outward together, toward their mission, their mission of love.

The family is a microcosm of the Church. At Mass, the Catholic (which literally means "Universal") Church comes together, face-to-face, to be strengthened by Christ and others, so as to reach out to all, especially the marginalized. The family strengthens each other and then reaches to help all, especially those most in need.

1. Your future marriage is to reach beyond your home. Discuss with each other what your family mission will mostly be geared toward. How will your love for each other blossom beyond the bed?

"[Each]… has received the other human being as a gift."   TOB 13:4

Submit to Christ!
You Can Trust Him

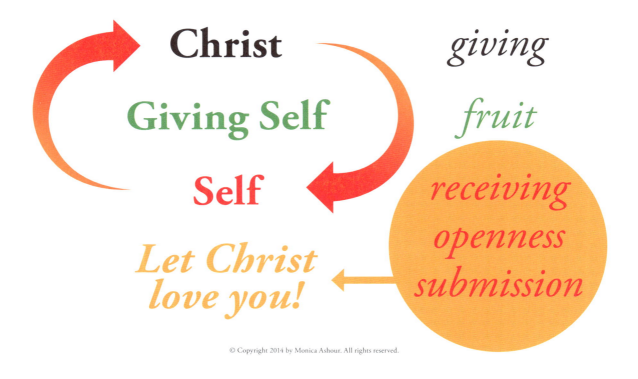

Mutual Submission
"Submit to one another out of reverence for Christ." Eph 5:22

We can only find ourselves in a truthful gift of self.
(See *Gaudium et Spes*, 24)

The male body says "initiate."

The female body says "receive."

Sacramentality of Marriage

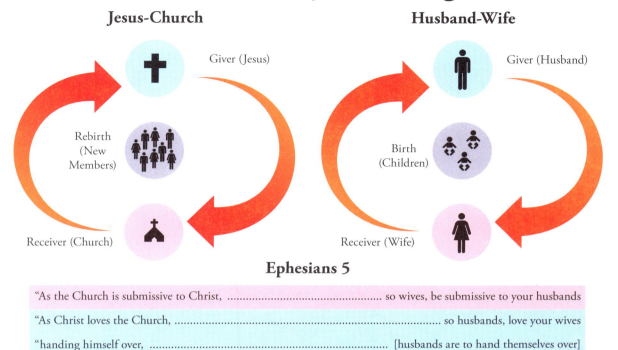

© Copyright 2014 by Monica Ashour. All rights reserved.

The word *submission* sometimes is taken wrongly to mean the husband makes uncompromising demands on his wife without taking into consideration his wife's opinion and feelings. St. Paul, however, tells us in Ephesians 5:21 to "Be mutually submissive"—to *receive* each other's unique gift and anticipate each other's need. The wife is to trust her husband in that she *receives* his sacrificial love—he is to die for her as Christ died for us.

Do you really want to know what marriage is about? Study the left side of this diagram: Take seriously what it means that on the Cross, Jesus the Bridegroom, the New Adam, gives Himself by *giving* Freely, Fully, Faithfully, and Fruitfully…and beneath the Cross, Mary who represents all of us as the Bride, the New Eve, gives herself by *receiving* Freely, Fully, Faithfully, and Fruitfully. What happened in Jerusalem on Calvary is the Wedding *par excellence*, which is "re-presented" at every Mass.

1. What do you think about *submission* being *accepting* or *receiving* someone's loving gift of self?

2. Do you work on *submitting* to Jesus' love for you?

3. What signs in your relationship now point to mutual submission and reciprocal reverence, first to Christ and the Church and then to each other?

4. Future wife: Do you think you will lovingly receive this man? Do you think he is trustworthy of receiving your vulnerable gift? Does he model Christ? Do you think he is capable of laying down his life completely for you? If so, what signs point to this in him? If not, what should you do about it?

5. Future husband: Do you think you are worthy of the vulnerable trust this woman places in you (are you ready to die for her, especially daily)? Do you think she is capable of receiving your vulnerable gift of laying down your life? Does she model Mary? If so, what signs point to this in her? If not, what should you do about it?

"We do not forget that the one and only key for understanding the sacramentality of marriage is the spousal love of Christ for the Church (see Eph 5:22-23)." — TOB 81:4

How Do You View the Body and Sex?

Body is Used	Body as Sacrament	Body is Feared
Body is a tool for pleasure or a means of power over another.	Body reveals the depth of my/your unique "I" in the truth of masculinity or femininity, made for love.	Body is a necessary evil; only my soul matters. Lack of attentiveness to feminine beauty or masculine strength.
Sexual organs are for pleasure only.	Male sexual organ for initiating love. Female sexual organ for receiving love. Openness to procreation. Pleasure is a gift.	Sexual organs are necessary for procreation only.
Sexual intercourse for individual pleasure—mutual masturbation.	Sexual intercourse brings about mutual union which always includes openness to life, in the very depth of my "I" with your "I."	Sexual intercourse for procreation only.
Lust reigns, ready for the next sexual encounter for one's selfish pleasure.	Love is renewed, the whole of married life flourishes — the one-flesh union reflects the security of indissolubility.	"Duty" requires engaging in intercourse with my spouse.

This chart is based on Pope John Paul II's words about delving into the first chapters of Genesis to see "in nucleo" almost all elements of the analysis of man. (cf. *TOB* 3:1), as well as John Paul's discussion about the body being in the form of a sacrament (cf. *TOB* 87:5). © Copyright 2014 by Monica Ashour. All rights reserved.

The pendulum has swung—from shows like *Dick Van Dyke* and *Father Knows Best* whereby the *married* couple is depicted as sleeping at night in *separate* beds...to shows that depict one night stands as the norm. Sex has gone from being feared (right column) to being viewed as the ultimate (left column). Both are wrong. The middle column is the goal, seeing the body as a sacrament. Most of us have come from one extreme or the other regarding the view of the body and sex. Our parents play a tremendous role in our vision and understanding of love, marriage, and sex.

1. From what background did you come? That is, what column was the emphasis of your parents and how did that affect your understanding of the body and sexuality? From what background did your future spouse come?

2. How can you both move toward an integral understanding of the body as a sacrament so as to align yourselves with God's design?

"Nowadays Christianity of the past is often criticized as having been opposed to the body; and it is quite true that tendencies of this sort have always existed. Yet the contemporary way of exalting the body is deceptive. *Eros*, reduced to pure 'sex', has become a commodity, a mere 'thing' to be bought and sold, or rather, man himself becomes a commodity. This is hardly man's great 'yes' to the body. On the contrary, he now considers his body and his sexuality as the purely material part of himself, to be used and exploited at will."

Pope Benedict XVI, *God Is Love*, 5

Lust vs. Love

Lust	Love
Is directed toward self-**gratification**	Is directed toward self-**donation**
Sees the body as some**thing**	Respects the body as some**one**
Sacrifices **others for oneself**	Sacrifices **oneself for others**
Grasps at **fleeting** pleasure	Yearns for **eternal** joy
Enslaves us	**Liberates** us
Manipulates and controls	**Respects** people's freedom
Is aimed at **any** pleasing outlet	Is reserved for **one and only**
Is aimed at **repeatable "qualities"**	Is aimed at the **unrepeatable person**

Diagram by Christoper West, MTS. Used with permission. © Copyright 2013 by Monica Ashour. All rights reserved.

You are in love! You would never *deliberately* use each other in a lustful way. A man once told me, "Until the theology of the body, I had no idea I had lusted after my own wife. I was disgusted and asked God to cleanse me. He did." Ask God for a pure heart of love. Ask and you will receive.

1. Freedom is often seen as doing whatever I want. True freedom lies in being able to love. In your future marriage, how will you both be diligent in steering away from lust to freedom for love?

"Love is indeed 'ecstasy', not in the sense of a moment of intoxication, but rather as a journey, an ongoing exodus out of the closed, inward-looking self towards its liberation through self-giving, and thus towards authentic self-discovery and indeed the discovery of God: 'Whoever seeks to gain his life will lose it, but whoever loses his life will preserve it' (Lk 17:33), as Jesus says throughout the Gospels (cf. Mt 10:39; 16:25; Mk 8:35; Lk 9:24; Jn 12:25)."

Pope Benedict, *God is Love*, 6

"[O]nly the chaste man and the chaste woman are capable of true love. For chastity frees their association, including their marital intercourse, from the tendency to use a person which is objectively incompatible with loving kindness, and by so freeing it introduces into their life together and their sexual relationship a special disposition to loving kindness."

Pope John Paul II, *Love and Responsibility*, 171

Avoid Adultery in All Its Forms

	Adultery		Marital Fidelity
Pornography	"Seeing a naked human body makes me crave sex!"	**Faithfulness**	"A naked human body is the revelation of a person, whom I am only to reverence, and never lust after."
Masturbation	"My body is an amusement park and sex is fun; I don't need anyone else for my sexual pleasure."	**Faithfulness**	"My body is a temple and sex is holy; I will enjoy sexual pleasure only with my spouse."
Flirting	"Arousing sexual feelings with other people is harmless fun!"	**Faithfulness**	"Sexual feelings are deeply important. I will arouse them only with and toward my spouse."
Cheating	"Sex means whatever I want it to mean, including a fling that means nothing at all."	**Faithfulness**	"Since sex with a person means I'm married to that person, I will only have sex with my spouse."

Created by Steve Patton, M.A., J.D. Used with permission. © Copyright 2015 by Monica Ashour. All rights reserved.

Naked & Unashamed vs. Pornographic Nudity

"…the man and his wife were both naked, and they felt no shame." Gen 2:25

"…anyone who looks at a woman lustfully has already committed adultery with her in his heart." Mt 5:28

Within Marriage
My wife is a complete person, so much more than just a beautiful body

I know her name…
I know her family…
I know her hopes and dreams…

Pornography
Her body is just a beautiful physical object for my pleasure

I don't care to know her name
I don't know her family
I don't care about who she is

Based on TOB 63:5. © Copyright 2014 by Monica Ashour. All rights reserved.

XXX is A.A.A.

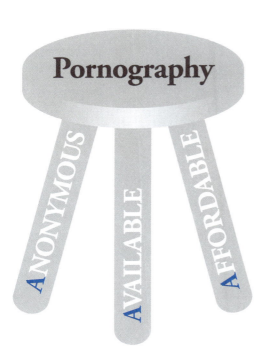

Resources for Self-Mastery

✔ **Covenant Eyes software**
Filters internet on computers and cell phones with an accountability system

✔ *Treating Pornography Addiction*
Non-religious book by Dr. Kevin B. Skinner

✔ **Support groups and accountability partners**

✔ **Healing and grace**
Through the Sacraments of Confession and Holy Communion

✔ **Pastoral support**

✔ **Professional counseling**

✔ **Reception of the Sacraments**

© Copyright 2014 by Monica Ashour. All rights reserved.

RESOURCES: *Learn the Detrimental Effects and Be Healed of Pornography*

My House Initiative, Kansas City, Archbishop Naumann and Sam Meier
www.diocese-kcsj.org/content/offices_and_agencies/my_house

Pornography is often overlooked… affecting modern life
www.usccb.org/issues-and-action/marriage-and-family/natural-family-planning/resources/pornography.cfm

Pornography's Effects on Marriage and the Hope of Recovery
www.foryourmarriage.org/the-effects-of-pornography-on-marriage/

Protecting Youth from Pornography
www.usccb.org/issues-and-action/child-and-youth-protection/resources/upload/InternetPornography-Slattery.pdf

Neurological Impact of Pornography
www.usccb.org/about/pro-life-activities/respect-life-program/2012/life-matters-pornography-and-our-call-to-love.cfm

Interfaith Statement about Pornography
www.usccb.org/beliefs-and-teachings/ecumenical-and-interreligious/jewish/upload/Joint-Statement-on-Pornography.pdf

Women and Online Pornography
www.foryourmarriage.org/women-and-online-pornography/

Restoring the Glory (Sexual Wholeness), Dr. Bob Schuchts
A powerful 5-Day Retreat, which includes healing of identity, wounds, compulsions, leading to freedom and integration.
www.jpiihealingcenter.org

To Love or To Use

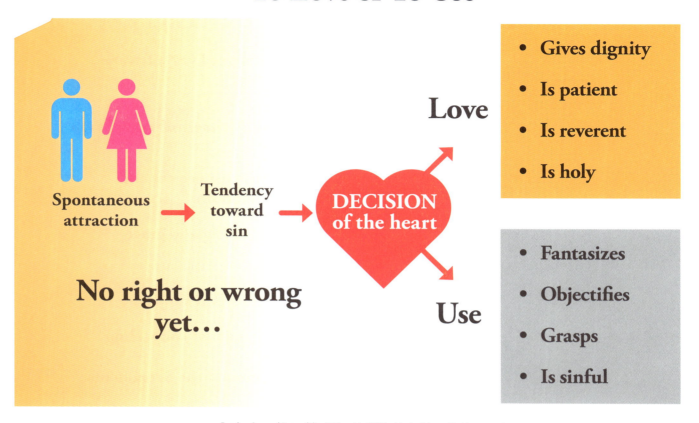

Based on *Love and Responsibility*. © Copyright 2014 by Monica Ashour. All rights reserved.

THE INNER MOVEMENTS OF THE HEART...

Do you love her... or her body as an object?

Is this for me... or him/her or us?

What is best for him/her?

Men are more physically charged...how do I take my wife into consideration?

Women are more emotionally charged...how do I take my husband into consideration?

1. When considering your past, have you used another or have you been used sexually in the past? How might that affect your future marriage? Are you in need of healing in this area?
2. What needs to happen to ensure sex as love, not sex as use in your relationship?

"Purification of the heart demands prayer, the practice of chastity, purity of intention and of vision."
CCC 2532

"[In marital intercourse] the other person is more important than 'I'." — John Paul II

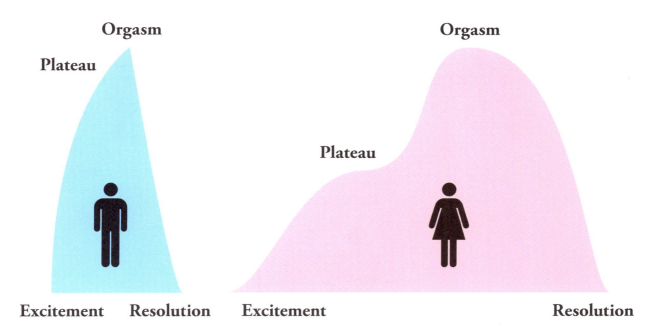

Based on *Love and Responsibility*, page 274. © Copyright 2013 by Monica Ashour. All rights reserved.

Pope John Paul says in *Love and Responsibility* that it is the responsibility of the husband to wait on the slow arousal curve of his wife; otherwise, rigidity toward her husband regarding intercourse may occur. He also speaks about sexual climax occurring simultaneously as an ideal. Nevertheless, the ultimate goal is communion with one's spouse throughout one's entire married life with intercourse as one expression of that reality.

1. What do you think about a Pope speaking openly about orgasm? Why would he give such advice regarding your marriage?

"…Men and women, as the act of making love shows, are not rivals in a power struggle, but partners—complementary partners—in a joint urge for self-abandon that makes them putty in each other's hands. Orgasm is a high point of reciprocal self-giving love. But the self-giving is different for the two spouses, different in ways that are not trivial and that cannot be overlooked. The chief difference is in male initiation and female receptivity.…But his initiation is not aggressive and oppressive…And her receptivity is not passive and degrading."

Mary Rouseau *"Pope John Paul II's Teaching on Women"*

3 FAITHFUL

TOBET4ENGAGED   53

What is the NUMBER ONE Virtue Needed in Marriage?

Man—what a woman! She's totally worth pursuing!

Initial Meeting

Whoa—he's amazing! I want him to notice me!

REVERENCE

Deepening Relationship

My crush is over, but she's still fascinating!

He has his weaknesses, but I'm still in awe of him!

© Copyright 2014 by Monica Ashour. All rights reserved.

Why is reverence *the foundational* virtue needed in marriage? Reverence is a way of honoring, showing awe toward, and respecting your future spouse as a person. The sometimes true adage, "Familiarity breeds contempt" is countered by reverence. When we first have reverence for God, then all His creation (especially your spouse!) will be treated properly. For instance, reverence is submitting to the body—not violating its normal processes—like the husband taking into account the woman's cycle and how that affects her emotionally. Or on the other side, the wife reverences her husband by taking into account his physically-charged sexual desire. And beyond the bedroom, in various life experiences, you can reverence your future spouse by being considerate, by empathizing, by seeing him/her as unique. This makes for a happy marriage.

1. What are ways you reverence each other now? How can you improve?

2. What are practical ways you will maintain reverence in your future married life?

"A man must take into account that a woman is a 'world different' from him, not only in the physiological, but also the psychological sense. Since he is to play an active role in conjugal intercourse, he should get to know this world, and even empathize with it as much as possible. This is precisely the positive function of tenderness. Without it, a man will attempt merely to subordinate a woman to the demands of his body and his psyche, at times acting to her detriment. Of course, a woman, too, should attempt to understand a man and at the same time to educate him in relation to herself, for one is not less important than the other. Neglect with respect to one of them can be equally a fruit of egoism."

Pope John Paul II, *Love and Responsibility*

The Crucible of Marriage

Rough edges are smoothed through daily living out the virtues with your spouse.

changing
giving
compromising
yielding
deferring

The fruit of the Spirit is love, joy, peace, patience, kindness, generosity, faithfulness, gentleness, self-control.
Gal 5:22

Based on John Paul II's *TOB* 50–57. © Copyright 2014 by Monica Ashour. All rights reserved.

"He will purify the sons of Levi and refine them like gold and silver, so that they may present to the LORD offerings in righteousness."

Malachi 3:3

Faithfulness to each other in all of family life will be difficult. If tainted gold could talk while it is in the purifying flame of fire, surely it would say, "GET ME OUT! I can't handle this." Most married couples from time to time will experience this feeling. The "throw-away culture," as Pope Francis likes to call it, would abandon ship, get out of the crucible of marriage, and turn away from sacrificial love which purifies. You will have the opportunity to yield, give, forgive, compromise... change. We resist change like the plague because change hurts. Yet, the Power of the Holy Spirit can break through, to smooth out your and your spouse's rough edges. Joy ensues.

1. The current "cute and endearing idiosyncrasies" of your beloved sometimes become sources of annoyance after marriage. Do you both pledge to go through purification? How so?

2. Sometimes the tough times of marriage are so serious, you may need an outsider to help guide you to solutions. Are you both open to going to counselling, if necessary, to work on strengthening—or saving— your marriage? Why or why not?

Cosmic Vision of Marriage

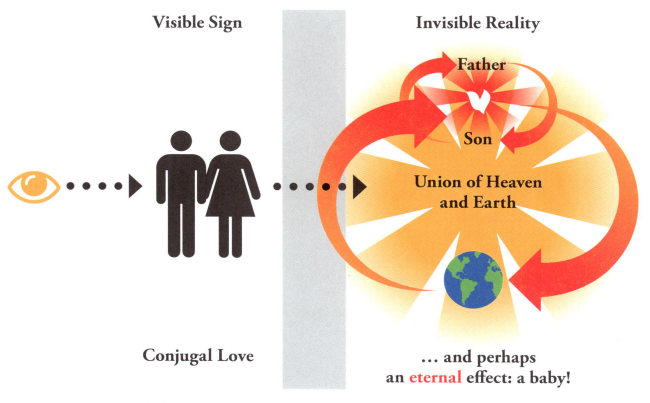

Based on *TOB* 13:2-4; 16:3-19:6; 93:1-7; 117b:6. © Copyright 2014 by Monica Ashour. All rights reserved.

What was God thinking when he decided that we mere humans can have actions which can have cosmic, eternal consequences!?! What power and privilege God gives to you as a couple! Love is the most powerful force in the universe. And conjugal love that is free, full, faithful, and fruitful is so powerful that heaven is brought to earth and a person (if conception occurs) can be brought to God for eternity. Such is the power God entrusts to you in your spousal love. Wow!

God will give you the power to be *faithful* to your vows, *faithful* to each other, *faithful* to your family in the day-to-day trials and joys of life. Remember, your communion of persons is based on God's very inner life of love and fidelity.

1. What strikes you about love bringing the Blessed Trinity to bear on the earth?

2. Have you ever thought of the fact that a baby conceived through intercourse changes the universe eternally? Discuss this amazing fact.

3. If people understood the sacredness of marital intercourse, do you think it would change this sex-saturated culture? If so, how? If not, why not?

4. How can this vision impact your upcoming marriage?

PART 4

The Gift of Love is FRUITFUL
OUR LOVE OVERFLOWS INTO THE LIVES OF OTHERS

God's Very First Command: Have Sex!

"Be fruitful and multiply"
Gen 1:28

Based on *TOB*. © Copyright 2013 by Monica Ashour. All rights reserved.

Free, full, faithful, and now *fruitful*! These aspects of love intertwine, like harmony and melody, like colors in a painting, like letters making words, like numbers making equations: without each piece, the beauty would be diminished and the gift incomplete.

Recall the diagram of God's Inner Life of Love. The Father and Son reciprocally give freely, fully, faithfully; and there IS a Person, the third Person of the Blessed Trinity. The Love of the three Persons of the Trinity is the blueprint for all love. Love is expansive. Love that walls up safe barriers shutting others out will eventually dry up.

Sheldon Vanauken writes a heart-rending love story, *A Severe Mercy*, about this truth when he retells the story of his marriage. (A fantastic book for engaged couples!) He and his wife loved each other so much that they did not want any children, for they saw children as having the potential to *divide* them. They erected what they called a "Shining Barrier," and even deliberately dented their brand new car so that *it* would not divide them. What noble sentiments they had...until they experienced the love of God, moving from atheism to Catholicism. They understood more clearly then their noble, yet wrong, ideal regarding children and all of creation. They realized that their love was meant to go out, not to be kept locked up and exclusive. They discovered that when love is true, it is open to others. True love is necessarily *fruitful*.

ABC vs. NFP

Though both can be used to avoid conception... there are big differences!

Artificial Birth Control	Natural Family Planning
Some **dangerous** side effects	**No** side effects
Couples have **less** sex	Couples have **more** sex
"I give you **only some** of me."	"I give you **all** of me."
No sacrifice required	Requires **sacrifice of self-mastery**
Mentality leads to **use of the other**	Mentality enlarges true **love of the other**
Prevents conception unnaturally	Conception is naturally **impossible**
Thwarts God's natural design	**Works with** God's natural design
The "**conquest** of nature"	**Submits** to nature
Interpersonal communication **not** needed	Requires **ongoing** communication
Closed to life	**Open** to life
Some types cause an **abortion**	Accepts life as **good**
Couple in control	**Couple and God** cooperate
The Pill is **carcinogenic** (per World Health Organization)	**Healthy** (no pills)
Lack of prayer	Part of **conjugal spirituality**

© Copyright 2014 by Monica Ashour. All rights reserved.

"So-called 'safe sex,' which is touted by the 'civilization of technology,' is actually, in view of the overall requirements of the person, radically not safe, indeed it is extremely dangerous. It endangers both the person and the family. What is this danger? It is the loss of truth about one's own self and about the family, together with the risk of a loss of freedom and consequently of a loss of love itself."

John Paul II, *Letter to Families*, 13

"Why did I not hear this before?!" is the typical response we hear from engaged couples, and even married couples, regarding the breathtaking teaching that St. John Paul calls "conjugal spirituality." Conjugal spirituality is a fancy phrase meaning that free, full, faithful, and fruitful marital love will be an unbelievable, secure experience of union; it will truly be the entire person encountering the entirety of the other in a mysterious way. What happens in this relationship is so unique and sacred, it is in a sense a liturgical act, that is, an act that gives glory and worship to God.

St. John Paul's concern is to safeguard this loving encounter. As a young priest who counseled so many couples, he found that contraception paved the way for *using* the other person—the opposite of love. Through contraceptive methods, the body began to be seen, not as a sacrament revealing the person, but as a shell and an object for expediting pleasure at all costs. This view leads to an exploitation of women.

Contraception Distorts the Meaning of the Body

Issue	Telling a Lie against the Body	Telling the Truth with the Body
Fertility	"We are 'conquering' our bodies to prevent the consequences of sex."	"I am pregnant! My body will 'shut down' everything else and prepare for motherhood."
The Pill	"Fertility is a disease and an impediment to pleasure whenever we want it."	"Her cycle is a sign to us that she is made for love for communion—first with each other; then with the possible baby."
"Protection"	"We are afraid—we might give each other a disease; a baby would make huge demands of us."	"We don't need 'protection' from those we love. Chastity guarantees freedom from disease. We are not afraid of sacrificial love since 'perfect love casts out all fear.'"
Condom	"This barrier means we refuse to give our full selves and refuse to accept our full selves, especially our fertility. We do NOT give fully."	"In the most intimate bodily act, we give our full selves and accept our full selves, including our fertility. We give FULLY."
Sex	"We don't need to be open to life; we are consenting adults; our sex won't hurt anyone. We will trade 'conjugal spirituality' for temporary pleasure."	"Contraception paves the road to use, the opposite of love. We express the deep meaning of sex, 'I am yours and you are mine freely, fully, faithfully, and fruitfully' and enjoy 'conjugal spirituality' as well."
Person	"We are objects of manipulation. Our bodies are not sacraments of us."	"NFP in marital love reverently safeguards and expresses our person-to-person deep communion."
God	"We thwart God's natural design."	"We embrace God's natural design."

Based on the Good of NFP and the Evil of Contraception in the TOB Chapter, "He Gave Them the Law of Life as their Inheritance." *TOB* 118-133. © Copyright 2014 by Monica Ashour. All rights reserved.

Pope John Paul says that Jesus' words are not words of condemnation but of invitation, an invitation to lasting love and fidelity in marriage, open to the richness of children.

NFP or "fertility awareness" is based on the ability of a woman/couple to identify the times of fertility and of infertility during each cycle with 99% degree of accuracy. Different methods have been developed in order to facilitate this process of discovering times of fertility and infertility. This study of the woman's reproductive cycle and the research invested in the development of fertility awareness methods have led to other medical advances such as those used in NaPro Technology™ (Natural Procreative Technology).

Thus, those couples who discern they need to limit their family size are aware of the proper times of abstinence and of union. This keeps the integrity of the truth of the body and the person intact, though it demands self-mastery, especially from the husband.

1. What makes sense about this teaching? What reaction do you have? How hard will it be for you to discuss this topic with your future spouse?

> "Since women literally embody receptivity, a loss of esteem for this dimension of humanity as a whole led to a loss of esteem for women."
>
> Servais Pinckaers,
> *"The Sources of Christian Ethics"*

> "The liturgical language assigns love, faithfulness, and conjugal integrity to both man and woman through the 'language of the body.'
>
> It assigns them the unity and indissolubility of marriage in the 'language of the body.'"
>
> Pope John Paul II, *TOB* 117b:2

4 FRUITFUL

Why Would I Deliberately Damage My Body?

Damaging action	Is my body hurting or sick? Yes	No	Reason for the action
Foot amputation	✔		To save my leg, if gangrene is present—in favor of life
Hysterectomy	✔		To prevent excessive bleeding or cancer—in favor of life
Tonsillectomy	✔		To prevent repeated infection or pain—in favor of life
Mastectomy	✔		To save my life, if cancer is present—in favor of life
Ligation ("tubes tied")		✘	To have sex without possibility of a child—against life
Vasectomy ("get clipped")		✘	To have sex without possibility of a child—against life

Natural family planning works with the body and *does not damage* the body.

It does require self-mastery, which is a good. Discipline and sacrifices *strengthen love.*

© Copyright 2014 by Monica Ashour. All rights reserved.

Another thing that people often don't think through is sterilization. We would think it absurd to deliberately cut off a perfectly functioning hand or gouge out an eye. Yet, when it comes to doing damage to our sexual organs, we forget. Our bodies are not shells—they are integral to us.

One of my friends told me with great sadness in his voice, "I knew getting a vasectomy was wrong, but I was worried about my wife's health. I did it for a good reason, but I know the end does not justify the means... and our marriage suffered."

Another woman told me with tears how she felt after her sterilization, sitting in the hospital bed, feeling empty, regretting her decision, wanting to be a mom again.

And later in life, when she told her adult child about the sterilization, he said to her, "Mom, was I such a burden that you wanted no more children?"

1. Most people have never thought about sterilization as a negative. What do you think about these stories? What does your future spouse think?

There's a sure way of not getting pregnant. Abstinence.
It may seem old-fashioned, but we can also call it "green": respecting, not damaging, creation.

SPICE Up Your Marriage!

Spiritual
- Read Bible
- Pray together

Physical
- Exercise
- Cuddling

Intellectual
- Online lectures
- Current events

Creative
- Home projects
- Music and dance

Emotional
- Plan for the future
- Share stories

Based on concepts from Dr. Hilgers and from Joanne Washburn. © Copyright 2014 by Monica Ashour. All rights reserved.

Some ask: "What is the difference between practicing natural family planning and artificial birth control? After all, both are used to prevent pregnancy." **A great question.**

First, let's note that natural family planning can also be used to *achieve* a pregnancy when infertility has been a problem. Moreover, some couples simply enjoy the idea of knowing the woman's fertility so that they know exactly when they will be pro-creators with God when they conceive a child.

But what about when the goal of not having a child is the same for both those practicing NFP and those using contraception? Actually, it may look like the goal is the same, but really, the couple that practices natural family planning has a goal of honoring nature, safeguarding love, and experiencing the spouse freely, fully, faithfully, and fruitfully whenever they come together in the marital embrace.

Think about it: who says a couple *has* to come together on days of fertility? No one. They choose to submit to the truth of the body, honoring the God-given fertility of the couple by abstaining in the woman's fertile times, usually less than a week out of her cycle.

When they do come together, she still gives her full self; she just doesn't have fertility to give since she is infertile.

We hear about so many couples who did not know the "why's behind the what's" of the Church's teaching who take a leap of faith and stop contracepting. They know NFP is not easy. Yet, they then experience a gift: their communication improves, their love blossoms, and their monthly "honeymoon time" becomes even more delightful, coming together again in conjugal intercourse after practicing abstinence with SPICE enriching their marriage. Being Christ-centered leads to happiness, even if sacrificial love is demanding.

1. What are some ways you as a couple enjoy expressing love for each other outside of the bedroom? What do you like to do together?

2. Could the Church be right that contraception lends itself to use, while NFP preserves Love?

3. Isn't it worth looking into it?

What is Your View of Children?

Commodity	Blessing
Financial drain	No price tag! (require sacrifice)
Burden	Gifts (and hard work)
Emotionally taxing	Sense of belonging (and toleration!)
Hard to control	Hard not to love (mystery of others with free will)
Cause resentment and trouble	Bring inspiration (and challenges)
Major carbon footprint	Give more than take
Unwanted intruders in a planned life	Icons of the Incarnation
Discretionary life-style choice	The supreme gift of marriage

Shall we over-analyze—or risk a fuller, richer, more complicated life?

© Copyright 2015 by Monica Ashour. All rights reserved.

"Behold, children are a heritage from the Lord, the fruit of the womb a reward."

Psalm 127:3

The Culture of Death has engrained in us a mentality that children are a burden. God never sees us as a burden—shouldn't we view children as He does...as gifts?

We might also note that a *gift* is very different from a *commodity*. Well-intentioned people go to great lengths to produce children using unnatural methods. The wife becomes pregnant not by her husband but by a doctor's instrument. Many unborn babies are unnaturally kept in a frozen state or "discarded" as if they were not persons. Once again, there is no judgment here; we mention this to help you think through the reality of *in vitro* fertilization or surrogacy.

When I worked as a campus minister at St. Mary's at Texas A&M, I recommended NaPro Technology to three different young married couples who struggled with fertility. All three had a simple procedure which cured the problem, and they conceived. The cost: financially, very little compared to sometimes over $10,000 for other procedures; morally, joy in following God's law.

I was brought to tears recently when I saw my friends—a married couple who are infertile—interact with their newly adopted daughter. Sheer joy!

1. Which column reflects my view of children and why do I experience children as such?
   Which column reflects my future spouse's view of children and why?

2. Are our views of children compatible with each other's? Compatible with God's?

Manufacturer vs. Pro-Creator

Wanting a child (good motive)

Wanting to be good, loving parents (good motive)

Conquering Nature	Honoring Nature
Child is manufactured product in test tube or in "surrogate"	Son or daughter co-created fruit in loving act
Produced outside of natural means	Conceived within natural order and received as a gift
Taking reproduction into one's own hands	Working within God's design of creation
Sometimes, the child does not know his/her mom and/or dad	The son or daughter has the security of knowing his/her family of origin
The child is objectified and seen as a "right" that is owed	Son or daughter is seen as the subject of his/her own life

Note: No matter how a child came into being, he or she is a person, to be respected and loved. Many well-meaning people, Catholic and non-Catholic alike, have never thought through the ramifications of in vitro fertilization and of surrogate motherhood. The truth of the body and sex, upheld by Scripture and Tradition, is shared here in the spirit of pastoral instruction, not judgment. For more information, contact a clinic using NaPro Technology like the National Center for Women's Health in Omaha, Nebraska; these centers work within God's design to overcome infertility.

This chart is based on TOB 20:1-2 which reflects on Genesis 4:1-2, on the *Catechism of the Catholic Church* 2376-2379, and on the Chief Rabbi of France, Gilles Bernhein's article (based on JP II's works) entitled "Homosexual Marriage" in *First Things Magazine*, May 2013. © Copyright 2014 by Monica Ashour. All rights reserved.

"Whoever receives one such child in my name receives me..." –Jesus, Mark 9:37

Adoption: A Beautiful Way of Being Fruitful

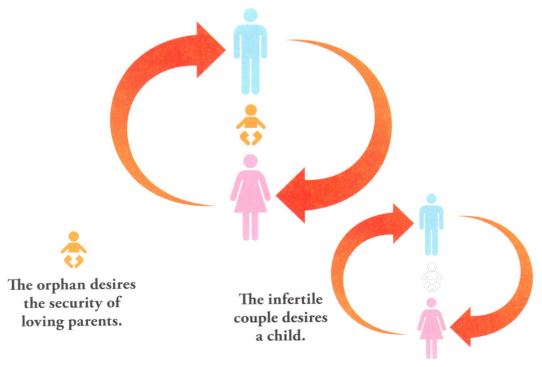

The orphan desires the security of loving parents.

The infertile couple desires a child.

Based on *CCC* 2379. © Copyright 2014 by Monica Ashour. All rights reserved.

Responsible Parenthood
Number and Spacing of Children

Extreme:	"Just Cause"	Extreme:
We decide without God	*Couple decides with God using reason, prayer, and respect for God-given fertility*	*God decides without us*
Any contraception is right		Even NFP is wrong
Violates human nature, especially fertility		Violates human nature, especially reason

Duty toward God, yourselves, your kids (current & future), society, the Church, and even humanity as a whole.

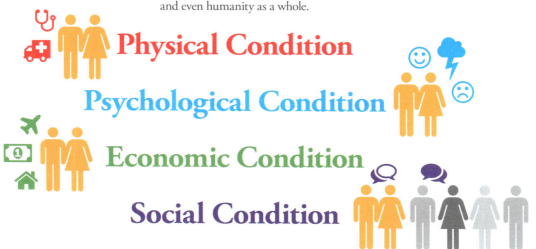

Physical Condition

Psychological Condition

Economic Condition

Social Condition

Based on *TOB* 121:2 & 125:3; *Humanae Vitae* 16; *Gaudium et Spes* 50. © Copyright 2014 by Monica Ashour. All rights reserved.

Marriage is not just about one person or even just about the two spouses. Rather, it is about the whole family and the influence that marriage and family life have beyond the walls of the home. For this reason, the Church has given some guidelines to think and pray about when deciding on the number of children to have. Many couples we know use NFP to limit their families, having only three children because a serious matter arises, including severe post-partum depression, loss of job due to an injury, or care for a special needs child, like my nephew, Nicky. Couples might discern that they need to limit their family size. Yet, we know other couples, including one with children with special needs, who believe they are called to have a bigger family. There is no magic number that the Church gives; instead, the Church gives the instruction that such a decision should be based on the common good and taken seriously.

1. Have you talked to each other about openness to a large family? What do you think? What does your future spouse think?

2. What does it mean that one's duty toward one's children (current and future) should be taken into consideration? What about one's duty toward the Church, God, or the rest of society?

"Love is demanding. It makes demands in all human situations; it is even more demanding in the case of those who are open to the Gospel. Is this not what Christ proclaims in 'his' commandment? Nowadays people need to rediscover this demanding love, for it is the truly firm foundation of the family, a foundation able to 'endure all things.'"

John Paul II, *Letter to Families*, 14

Responsible Parenthood… for the Next Generation

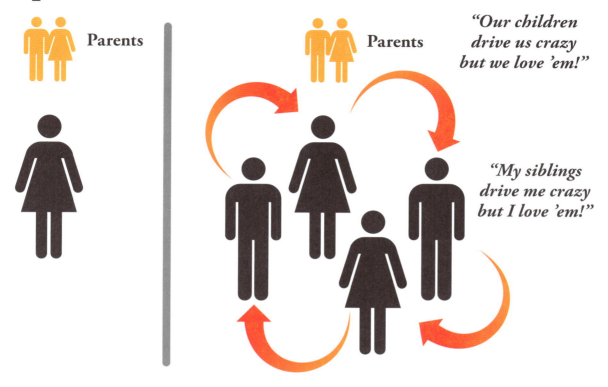

Your sacrifice today builds a better future for you — and your children

© Copyright 2013 by Monica Ashour. All rights reserved.

As we have discussed, children are not commodities; the number of children does not increase their individual goodness. Couples who struggle with fertility issues can bear fruit in different ways. It is worth considering, though, that as you make the sacrificial commitment to bear and raise children, siblings are a gift to each other, and the struggles to raise a large family can be rewarding.

1. Have you ever considered that by giving your children brothers and sisters, you are loving them? How will you take this reality into account in your number and spacing of children?

2. It is a blessing to have children, but sacrificial, demanding love is also part of it.
Discuss sacrifices that need to be made for the sake of your children's future.

"Thus the home is the first school of Christian life and 'a school for human enrichment.' Here one learns endurance and the joy of work, fraternal love, generous—even repeated—forgiveness, and above all divine worship in prayer and the offering of one's life." CCC 1657

Person-to-Person Encounter: Body

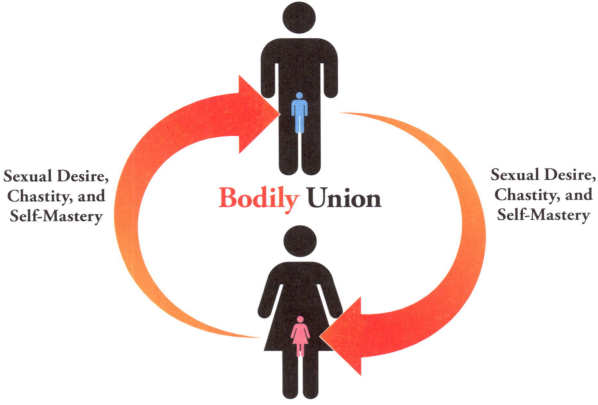

Based on Pope John Paul II's "Outline of Conjugal Spirituality," *TOB* 126-128. © Copyright 2014 by Monica Ashour. All rights reserved.

Person-to-Person Encounter: Emotions

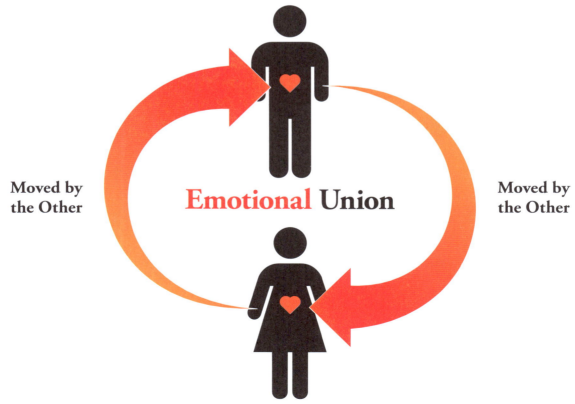

Based on Pope John Paul II's "Outline of Conjugal Spirituality," *TOB* 129:2-130. © Copyright 2014 by Monica Ashour. All rights reserved.

Person-to-Person Encounter: Spirit

Holy Spirit's Gift of Reverence

Spiritual Union

Holy Spirit's Gift of Reverence

Based on Pope John Paul II's "Outline of Conjugal Spirituality," *TOB* 131-132. © Copyright 2014 by Monica Ashour. All rights reserved.

"As proof that you are children, God sent the spirit of His Son into our hearts...."
Gal 4:6

One main reason St. John Paul wrote the theology of the body was that he saw the decay in the proper understanding of the human person, particularly regarding the body and sexuality, leading to sexual experiences emptied of love. In contrast, the true meaning of marital intercourse is that two complete people are to encounter each other: freely, fully, faithfully, and fruitfully. Through this encounter of their whole selves—body, soul, and spirit—they experience the wonder of loving and being loved in a fruitful communion. May you experience that in your marriage.

"The 'language of the body' speaks to the senses....The bride knows that 'his desire' is for her. She goes to meet him with the readiness of the gift of self. The love that unites them is of a spiritual and sensual nature together. On the basis of this love, the rereading of the spousal meaning of the body in the truth is achieved, because the man and the woman together must constitute the sign of the reciprocal gift of self, which sets the seal on their whole life." TOB 111:5

4 FRUITFUL

TOBET4ENGAGED

Person-to-Person Encounter: The Power of Love

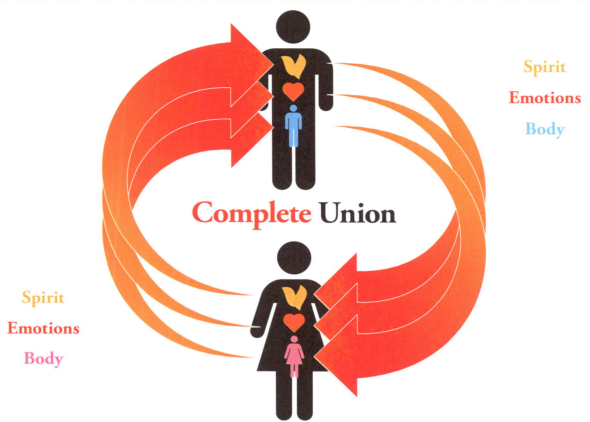

Based on Pope John Paul II's "Outline of Conjugal Spirituality," *TOB* 126-132. © Copyright 2014 by Monica Ashour. All rights reserved.

"May the God of peace himself make you whole—spirit, soul, and body." 1 Thessalonians 5:23

Just think! You and your fiancé/fiancée are about to embark on a journey of love! True love has power. It has the power to break through our wounds, our barriers, our weaknesses, to reveal the mystery of the person—the mystery of your spouse. In this way, true love brings about a person-to-person encounter and fulfills the deepest desire of the human heart.

1. The best marriages engage the whole person in the whole of family life. When you are married, how will you work to grow in each aspect of the whole person: body, soul, and spirit?

2. The "rules" of God, given to the Church, are not imposed from above. Rather, they are revealed from within, safeguarding true love for a communion of persons. Have you considered the "rules" as helping love to flourish? Is there a "rule" that you think hinders a person-to-person encounter? For more enrichment regarding the "why's behind the what's of the "rules" of the Church's teaching, see page 77.

"This gift [of reverence for what God has created] brings with it a deep and all-encompassing attention to the person in his or her masculinity or femininity, thus creating the interior climate suitable for personal communion."   TOB 132:5

PART 5

The Gift of Love Forms a FAMILY

"WE" BECOMING HOLY: LIVING THE TRUTH AS FAMILY

Vow to Vow: Baptismal Vow to Vocational Vow

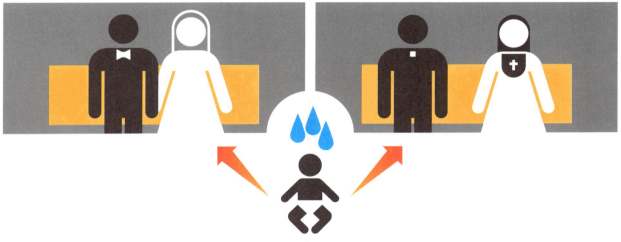

Vow of Marriage
"I promise to be true to you, my spouse, Freely, Fully, Faithfully and Fruitfully."

Vow of Celibacy for the Kingdom
"I promise to be committed to you, my Church, Freely, Fully, Faithfully and Fruitfully."

Vow of Baptism
"I promise to be committed to you, Jesus and Your Church, Freely, Fully, Faithfully and Fruitfully."

© Copyright 2014 by Monica Ashour. All rights reserved.

As parents, we have many responsibilities in raising our children "according to the law of Christ and His Church," as we professed when we took vows. Some include:

- Teaching them about God's love and Christianity
- Forming them in the Bible and in receiving the Sacraments
- Developing a personal relationship with Jesus with times of silence and prayer
- Helping them to see they are called by God to Holy Marriage, Holy Orders, or Holy Consecrated Life

1. How can you mirror God's great gift of unconditional love to your spouse and children?

2. What are concrete steps you will take to pass on the faith? Family catechesis? Catholic school? Religious education classes where you are the teacher? We recommend: "Catechesis of the Good Shepherd"

3. How will you and your future spouse teach your children about the holy vocations of marriage, priesthood, and religious life? How will you prepare your children for each of these vocations?

"The education of children should be such that when they grow up they will be able to follow their vocation, including a religious vocation, and choose their state of life with full consciousness of responsibility…"
Gaudium et Spes, 52

Strong Roots = Good Fruit

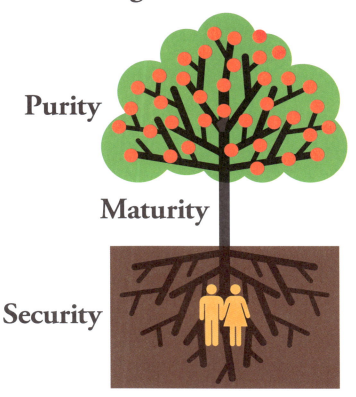

Starting at a young age, children are formed to be mature and pure adults when they are secure in the indissoluble love of their parents for each other.

Based on concepts from Dr. Bob Schuchts of The John Paul II Healing Center, Tallahassee, Florida. Used by permission. © Copyright 2014 by Monica Ashour. All rights reserved.

Children Need to Hear One Harmonized Voice

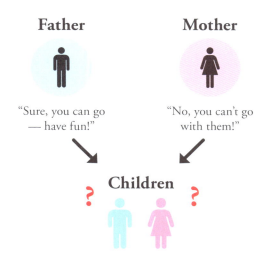

Children learn to manipulate their parents, causing division.

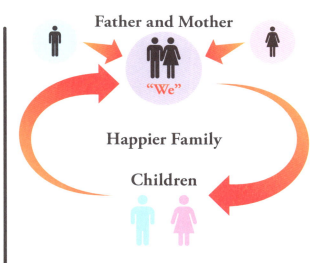

Children experience the security of a "united front," resulting in harmony.

On significant matters, parents can dialogue first in private to work out the best decision. For less important issues, however, resolving the disagreement in front of the children can give them greater security.

© Copyright 2014 by Monica Ashour. All rights reserved.

Stages of Sexual Development

Stage	Age	Learning Challenges
Attachment	0–2	***Developing secure love bonds with mother/father*** Learning to feel safe with same-sex and opposite-sex caregivers
Identification	3–5	***Identifying with same-sex parent*** and establishing a healthy bond with both parents Exploring opposite-sex attraction with opposite-sex parent
Peer group belonging	6–12	***Belonging with same-sex peer group*** Gender identity affirmed in peer relationships
Sexual exploration	13–22	***Learning how to develop opposite-sex relationships*** and channel sexual arousal and attraction Developing an integrated social and personal identity with our sexuality Learning self-mastery in becoming sexually chaste
Self-giving love	Adult	***Sexual fidelity and fruitfulness*** Living out sexual identity in intimate relationships in family and community as celibate or married persons Being fruitful in that love by procreating and caring for offspring (natural and spiritual children) Helping to shape sexual development of others as parents and parental figures

Based on concepts from Dr. Bob Schuchts of The John Paul II Healing Center, Tallahassee, Florida. Used by permission. © Copyright 2014 by Monica Ashour. All rights reserved.

Sex education for your children begins at a very early age—not that you speak explicitly to your two and four year olds about intercourse, but that you help them to see that certain bodily actions mean certain things. This Sacramental View of Reality that you are instilling in them forms their imaginations; it shows them that visible things matter, and that these visible things reveal and even bring about the truths that they signify.

Simply put, something like a kiss says, "I'm close to you as in a family" and it actually does what it symbolizes: strengthening familial bonds. You teach your child not to kiss strangers not because kissing is bad; it is because kissing *means* something: the people who share a kiss should be in close relationship. This sets a solid foundation for when it is the right time to give the talk on the "birds and the bees," preferably the dad telling his son and the mom her daughter. "Remember, son/daughter, that we taught you certain bodily actions mean certain things? Well, here's one you never want to empty of its meaning. There is something called sexual intercourse (describe it biologically, but never stop there without its deepest meaning). Sexual intercourse means, 'I'm married to you! I'm ready to become a parent with you!' It's the closest we can be to another human, which is why you wait until marriage—that's when you know you can trust each other forever." One talk, however, is insufficient, especially given the culture. Ongoing dialogue is crucial to your child's formation. Beyond forming your children in the area of sexual development and formation, you are meant to teach them about character, virtue, service, commitment, faith-life, sacrificial love, heaven, hell, forgiveness, and so much more—including play! Having fun is a human need!

1. How will you address the issues of sexuality with your children? Are you comfortable with such a discussion?

2. How will the information in the above chart be useful in raising your children to be healthy as they go through their psycho-sexual development?

"Human sexuality is a sacred mystery and must be presented according to the doctrinal and moral teaching of the Church, always bearing in mind the effects of original sin." *The Truth and Meaning of Human Sexuality*, 122

TOBET4ENGAGED 71

Gender Theory vs. She for Him/He for Her

The body has NO meaning	The body reveals DEEP meaning
Gen. 1:27: "God created man in his image; in the divine image he created him; MALE and FEMALE, he created them."	
My body can't tell me whether I am male or female. I decide, day-to-day, and I might change: today I am male/tomorrow female. (Note: Focus on the self with no recourse to the body)	My body tells me whether I am male or female. If I live according to the language of my body, I will know my identity and foster growth in my ability to love all. (Note: Focus on true identity so as to love others)
Genesis 2:18: "It is NOT good for man to be alone. I will make a suitable partner for him."	
My body has nothing to do with being in relationship with others; I am an autonomous self. I need no one. I need to try out many partners to find what works for me.	The complementarity of the male body and the female body has deep meaning: we are made FOR the other; love is the meaning of life. My body tells me that a one-flesh union is reserved for one, and one alone, indissolubly.
Genesis 2:23: "This one shall be called 'woman,' for out of 'her man' this one has been taken."	
There is no difference from one body to the next body; we are all the same.	It is glorious that all humans are made male or female: distinct yet equal in dignity as humans.
Gen. 2:25: "Therefore, a man shall leave his father and mother and cling to his wife, and the two shall become one body."	
Sexual encounters have little meaning; there should be no restrictions on consenting adults; Sex has nothing to do with commitment.	The sexual union of man and woman says, "I am yours and you are mine; we are one BODY forever, never to be dissected or divided."
Genesis 1:28: "Be fruitful and multiply."	
My body has nothing to do with propagating the species; maleness and femaleness are random. I have "reproductive rights" regardless of offspring that may result in intercourse. Babies have no rights.	The procreative potential of husband and wife as one body shows God's design for children to be conceived and raised in a loving atmosphere for security, a necessary ingredient for forming identity.

This chart is based on Pope John Paul II's words about delving into the first chapters of Genesis to see "in nucleo" almost all elements of the analysis of man. (cf. *TOB* 3:1).
© Copyright 2013 by Monica Ashour. All rights reserved.

Throughout this book, we have tried to convey the significance of the body as a sacrament of the whole person, and that the body has deep meaning, which guides us in our search for identity and purpose.

Proponents of gender theory tell us that our bodies do not guide us regarding the truth...we can simply decide what gender we are. Yet, our sex—as male or female—is based on the body and its meaning. As future parents, you are the most formative influences on your children. Although it will difficult to challenge prevalent ideologies (seen in Facebook's 50 gender options), help them to see the greater truth that the body matters, and to accept the body for what it is, a revelatory gift from God.

Meanwhile, teach them that every single person we encounter deserves a response of love. This is equally true for people who consider themselves to be the opposite gender from the sex of their bodies, or persons who say they are homosexual, transsexual, etc. Love is the only fitting response.

1. What strikes you about the chart above?

2. How will you handle a concrete circumstance of a family member or friend who experiences Same Sex Attraction? How will you stand firm in your Christian beliefs and be filled with joyful love of all?

"Our sexual identity extends to our souls, our personalities, our spirits. There is indeed a 'feminine mind' and a 'masculine mind' as well as body, for we are a psychosomatic unity (soul-body unity). To think of one's soul and mind as neither masculine or feminine is to separate body and soul artificially, as did the ancient Gnostics, and to think of the soul as a sexless 'ghost in a machine' instead of as the life and form of the body, and to think of masculinity and femininity as merely a material, animal thing."

Peter Kreeft, *Catholic Christianity*, Ch. 8, 4

"This is My Body"— The Eucharist as the Basis of Marriage

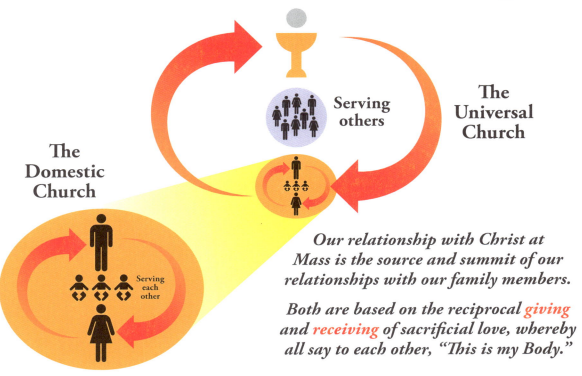

Our relationship with Christ at Mass is the source and summit of our relationships with our family members.

Both are based on the reciprocal *giving* and *receiving* of sacrificial love, whereby all say to each other, "This is my Body."

Based on *CCC* 2427 and *TOB* 131. © Copyright 2014 by Monica Ashour. All rights reserved.

The most important words of the universe are "THIS IS MY BODY, GIVEN," that is, *all* of me loves *all* of you—*sacrificially*.

As gifts to each other, family members form a "little church." Throughout my twenty plus years of teaching, I could readily spot a child whose parents loved each other. The best adjusted students were those who witnessed first-hand their parents' mutual love for one another. Often, those parents would tell me that they still had "date night" which remained a priority.

"As a gift and a commitment, children are their most important task." (The Pontifical Council's document, *The Truth and Meaning of Human Sexuality*, 51)

1. What practical steps will you take as a couple to be a model of mutual love for each other, forming a "united front" to give security to your children?

2. What concrete steps will you take to make your family a "home of faith and prayer"?

3. The father of a family is a crucial person in the formation of children. Men: Do you feel up to such a responsibility? Women: Do you think he will make a good father to your children? Why or why not? Give concrete examples.

4. The mother is seen as the "soul" of the family. Women: Do you feel up to such a responsibility? Men: Do you think she will make a good mother to your children? Why or why not? Give concrete examples.

"Lastly, we recall that in order to achieve these objectives, the family first of all should be a home of faith and prayer, in which God the Father's presence is sensed, the Word of Jesus is accepted, the Spirit's bond of love is felt, and where the most pure Mother of God is loved and invoked."

The Truth and Meaning of Human Sexuality, 62

Expectations!! Sources of Tension — or Sources of Union

On a scale of 1-5, with 5 being Totally Me and 1 being Totally Not Me, rate the following.

TOPIC: TIME

1. I'm almost always on time. — 1 2 3 4 5
2. Being prompt is a way of showing respect to another person. — 1 2 3 4 5
3. When I drive, I don't care if I am going slow even in the "fast" left lane. — 1 2 3 4 5
4. When we invite guests over for dinner, the meal should be ready when they arrive. — 1 2 3 4 5
5. I consider myself balanced regarding my view of time. — 1 2 3 4 5
6. It drives me crazy to be late for Mass or a wedding or another formal event. — 1 2 3 4 5
7. I'd prefer the fast-pace of New York to the slow pace of country life in Indiana. — 1 2 3 4 5
8. I'm a night owl. — 1 2 3 4 5
9. I need at least an hour to get ready to go anywhere. — 1 2 3 4 5
10. I expect a quick response to a text, email, or phone call. — 1 2 3 4 5

TOPIC: FUN!

1. I consider watching a movie at home a fun thing to do. — 1 2 3 4 5
2. If I don't get out of the house now and then, I tend to become depressed. — 1 2 3 4 5
3. Watching sports is quite fun for me. — 1 2 3 4 5
4. Having an elegant dinner causes more stress than fun for me since it costs so much money. — 1 2 3 4 5
5. Vacations with travel are overrated. I'd rather vacation at home, just being together. — 1 2 3 4 5
6. I prefer the beach over any other place. (If false, what are your favorite places for fun?) — 1 2 3 4 5
7. Basically, what I did growing up for fun is what I still like. (Explain what it is/isn't). — 1 2 3 4 5
8. When a fun outing is planned but someone cancels on me, I am extremely disappointed. — 1 2 3 4 5
9. Watching TV at home is one of my favorite forms of relaxation. — 1 2 3 4 5
10. Fun is just being with you. — 1 2 3 4 5

TOPIC: SPENDING

1. I'd prefer to get something tangible that lasts rather than spend money on an experience. — 1 2 3 4 5
2. A big vacation is my preference as opposed to small vacations for less money. — 1 2 3 4 5
3. Receiving flowers/tickets to sporting events rather than something useful is my preference. — 1 2 3 4 5
4. I'd rather save money and pay off our house before we go on elaborate vacations. — 1 2 3 4 5
5. Children are expensive, but I'd still like to have a large family. — 1 2 3 4 5
6. I like being really strict about a budget—come what may, we need to be in the black. — 1 2 3 4 5
7. I'd love it for you to make me a nice dinner at home than plan a get-away-weekend. — 1 2 3 4 5
8. I don't really have much of a preference about spending. — 1 2 3 4 5
9. I'd rather save money for college for our kids than send them to Catholic schools. — 1 2 3 4 5
10. I emulate my parents' spending habits. (Which are what?) — 1 2 3 4 5

CONCLUSION:
Marriage as the Mirror of the Gospel

BRINGING CHRIST TO THE WORLD THROUGH MARRIAGE

Your Marriage in the Big Picture

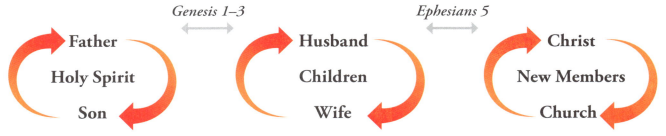

"So God created man in His own image, in the image of God He created him; male and female He created them." Gen 1:27

"Now as the Church submits to Christ, so also wives should submit to their husbands in everything. Husbands, love your wives, just as Christ loved the Church and gave Himself up for her…" Eph 5:24–25

© Copyright 2014 by Monica Ashour. All rights reserved.

"Everything of mine is yours and everything of yours is mine."
— The Son to the Father in John 17:10

As we conclude, let's remember the early diagram showing God's blueprint of love resulting in fruitful communion. Your future marriage, entering into Free, Full, Faithful, and Fruitful Love, will reflect God's blueprint: giving, receiving, returning, and being open to fruitfulness. You are to be the "best natural sign" to the world of God's plan for human love.

1. What concrete steps can you take in your day-to-day, often mundane tasks of your marriage and family life to ensure you are the "best natural sign" of reciprocal giving and receiving of free, full, faithful, and fruitful love?

2. Take the time to discuss this diagram and what it now means to you and your future marriage.

Your Marriage as the "Mirror" of the Gospel

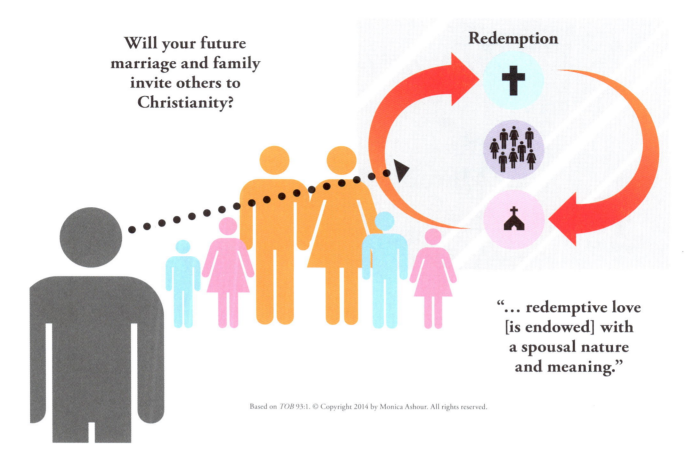

"… redemptive love [is endowed] with a spousal nature and meaning."

Based on *TOB* 93:1. © Copyright 2014 by Monica Ashour. All rights reserved.

The Blessed Trinity is the "first family." Christianity is the "universal" (or "Catholic") family. Your family, by providing a safe place for secure love to flourish, can bring others into God's family. Your marriage will have a profound impact on the world. Discuss how the strength (or weakness) of your marriage will affect the following:

1. Your spiritual, emotional, and physical well-being …and your future spouse's eternal well-being—you are to assist your spouse in getting to heaven.

2. Your future spouse's spiritual, emotional, and physical well-being…and your eternal well-being —your spouse is to assist you in getting to heaven.

3. The growth and development of your children in all of these areas.

4. Society at large, since your family is to bear witness to the Love of God.

"In our own time, in a world often alien and even hostile to faith, believing families are of primary importance as centers of living, radiant faith." CCC 1656

"The future of humanity passes by way of the family."

John Paul II, *The Role of the Christian Family in the Modern World*

4 Simple Steps to Staying Married…

Dr. Janet Smith promises $1,000 to couples who live these four principles, but then divorce.

"If you get God, sex, and money in the right place, everything else is easy."

Wait	Do not have sex before marriage. If you've started, stop… and start thinking about sex and what it's all about and why it's a good idea not to have sex before you get married.
Pray	When you get married, get married in a church, go to church every Sunday, pray while you're there, and live by the teachings of the church.
Plan	Use Natural Family Planning if you need to limit your family size.
Tithe	Give ten percent of your money to church or charity.

Based on Dr. Janet Smith's talk from www.janetsmith.excerptsofinri.com © Copyright 2014 by Monica Ashour. All rights reserved.

GOING DEEPER: *Resources for further growth*

Pope John Paul II
pauline.org
The Role of the Christian Family in the Modern World (A great, short summary of the theology of the body).

Pope Benedict XVI
pauline.org
God is Love

United States Council of Catholic Bishops
usccb.org
National Pastoral Initiative for Marriage; Marriage: Love and Life in the Divine Plan

Christopher West
christopherwest.com
Cor Project; *Fill These Hearts*

Dr. Janet E. Smith
janetsmith.org
Sexual Common Sense; Contraception: Why Not?

Dr. Peter Kreeft
peterkreeft.com *Heaven, the Heart's Deepest Longing; Catholic Christianity*

Dr. Bob Schuchts
jpiihealingcenter.org
Healing the Whole Person Seminar; *Be Healed*

Dr. Jennifer Roback Morse
ruthinstitute.org
101 Tips for Happier Marriages

Harville Hendrix & Helen LaKelly Hunt
harvillehendrix.com
Making Marriage Simple: Ten Simple Truths to a Happy Marriage; Imago Dialogue: 3 Steps to Connection

Jason & Crystalina Evert
chastityproject.com
Pure Manhood; Theology of His Body/Theology of Her Body; How to Find Your Soulmate Without Losing Your Soul

Greg and Julie Alexander
thealexanderhouse.org
Covenant of Love; Made for Each Other

Anastasia Northrop
NationalCatholicSingles.com
National Catholic Singles Conference

Jen Messing
idretreats.org
Into the Deep

National Center for Women's Health, Omaha, Nebraska
naprotechnology.com
Pope Paul VI Institute for the Study of Human Reproduction

Pontifical Council for the Family
vatican.va/roman_curia/ pontifical_councils/family/ index.htm
The Truth and Meaning of Human Sexuality

Monica Ashour
tobet.org

• TOBET Seminars (Workshops and specialized Certificates of Training in TOB for Youth Ministers, Marriage and Family Life Directors, Catechists, DREs, and Campus Ministers)

• *Project Family* (Age-appropriate Talks and Retreats for the Whole Family)

• *ToB for Tots* (Books for 1–4 year olds)

• *ToB for Kids* (Books for 5–8 year olds)

• Individual PowerPoint® presentations for Parents, for Educators, and for Teens on various topics

• *Parent's Guide to Theology of the Body for Teens: Middle School Edition*

END

TOBET4ENGAGED

It's All About Love

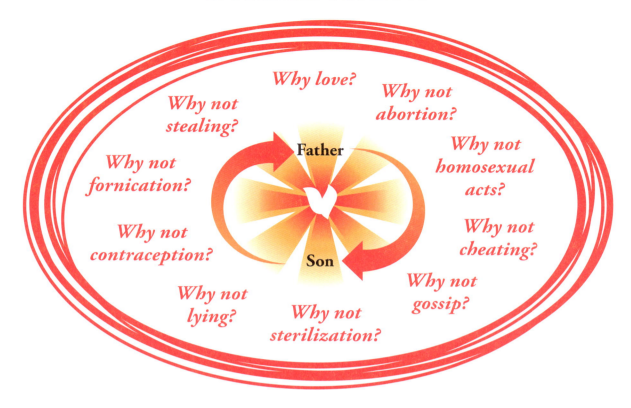

© Copyright 2014 by Monica Ashour. All rights reserved.

What a whirlwind this has been! TOBET's hope is that you will return to these truths and see how they are verified in your everyday life, your "hope for everyday," as Saint John Paul puts it.

As you have seen, his theology of the body is not a "No, no, no!" rulebook. Rather, St. John Paul the Great emphasizes the wondrous "Yes": "Yes to love," "Yes to sacrifice," "Yes to your beloved," "Yes to the sacredness of sex," "Yes to your children," "Yes to holiness" and…"Yes to the BODY"—"Yes to the *Incarnate* Body of Christ, the *Eucharistic* Body of Christ, and the *Mystical* Body of Christ, none other than you and your spouse."

May you, like our Mother Mary, say "Yes!" And just as by her "Yes!" the Word was made *flesh* in our world, so may your "Yes" of true and lasting love prove a great blessing to your mutual love, to your offspring, to the Church, and to the whole world.

*"Glory be to the Father, and to the Son, and to the Holy Spirit,
as it was in the beginning, is now, and ever shall be, world without end. Amen."*

Mother Mary and Pope Saint John Paul, pray for us!

"…[M]arriage [is] the most ancient revelation (and 'manifestation') of that plan in the created world with the definitive revelation and 'manifestation,' namely, the revelation that 'Christ loved the Church and gave himself for her' (Eph 5:25), endowing his redemptive love with a spousal nature and meaning." TOB 93:1

"Love [Agape] will never end."

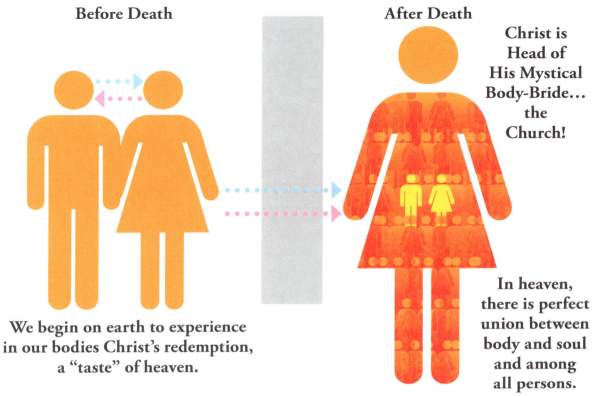

Before Death

We begin on earth to experience in our bodies Christ's redemption, a "taste" of heaven.

After Death

Christ is Head of His Mystical Body-Bride… the Church!

In heaven, there is perfect union between body and soul and among all persons.

Song of Songs 8:6, I Cor 13:8. Based on *TOB* 112–113. © Copyright 2014 by Monica Ashour. All rights reserved.

"Love is as strong as death."
— Song of Songs 8:6

The Power of the Holy Spirit

"…[Behind] these moral virtues stands a specific choice, that is, an effort of the will, a fruit of the human spirit permeated by the Spirit of God… man proves to be stronger thanks to the power of the Holy Spirit, who, working within the human spirit, causes its desires to bear fruit in the good."
TOB 51:6

Based on *TOB* 51. © Copyright 2013 by Monica Ashour. All rights reserved.

"God calls you to make definitive choices, and he has a plan for each of you: to discover that plan and to respond to your vocation is to move forward toward personal fulfillment. God calls each of us to be holy, to live his life, but he has a particular path for each one of us. Some are called to holiness through family life in the sacrament of Marriage.

Today, there are those who say that marriage is out of fashion. Is it out of fashion? In a culture of relativism and the ephemeral, many preach the importance of 'enjoying' the moment. They say that it is not worth making a life-long commitment, making a definitive decision, 'for ever,' because we do not know what tomorrow will bring.

I ask you, instead, to be revolutionaries, I ask you to swim against the tide; yes, I am asking you to rebel against this culture that sees everything as temporary and that ultimately believes you are incapable of responsibility, that believes you are incapable of true love.

I have confidence in you and I pray for you. Have the courage 'to swim against the tide.' And also have the courage to be happy."

Pope Francis, Sunday, July 28, 2013
Address to World Youth Day Volunteers

May the Holy Spirit guide you in your marriage and your future family life!